COACHING

The First Five Tools for Strategic Leaders

COACHING
The First Five Tools
for Strategic Leaders

Rick Mann, PhD

Coaching: The First Five Tools for Strategic Leaders
By Rick Mann, PhD

Published by: ClarionStrategy, LLC, Nashville, TN

www.ClarionStrategy.com
www.ClarionToolBox.com

DEDICATION

To all the leaders out there who are working hard to become the best version of themselves and for those who aspire to effectively coach others.

TABLE OF CONTENTS

ClarionToolBox Series

Strategic Leaders Are Made, Not Born: The First Five Tools for Escaping the Tactical Tsunami by Rick Mann, PhD

Building Strategic Organizations: The First Five Tools of Strategy and Strategic Planning by Rick Mann, PhD

Strategic Finance for Strategic Leaders: The First Five Tools by Rick Mann, PhD and David Tarrant, MBA

Enterprise Leaders: The First Five FIELD Tools (coming 2021) by Rick Mann, PhD and Dean Diehl

ACKNOWLEDGMENTS

Thanks to all the great coaches who have coached me over the years. Their guidance has not only benefited me personally and professionally, it has also helped those I have coached and trained to be coaches.

A special thanks to Mike Sohm, who is not only a great coach in his own right, but has also been an important professional colleague on coaching matters for over two decades.

I want to acknowledge the many coaching professionals who have personally coached me, trained me, or partnered with me in coaching endeavors, including the late Steve Ogne (CRM), Keith Webb (Creative Results Management), Greg Salciccioli (Coachwell), and Daniel Harkavey and Raymond Gleason (both at Building Champions). If you are looking for coaching help, I would recommend any of them to you.

I also want to thank Neil Sharpe, one of the most effective licensed counselors I have worked with, for the insights he has provided on some of these topics.

Any value I bring to coaching is in part because of the contributions these professionals have made to my coaching thinking and practice. Any weaknesses I bring to this work are solely my responsibility.

Thanks to skilled contributions and hard work from our series editor, Kara de Carvalho, and our series designer, Lieve Maas.

I must always acknowledge the enduring support of my wife, Cheri, who has helped me over the decades to become a better version of myself.

PREFACE

Coaching seems to be ubiquitous these days as people talk about how many are becoming coaches and how just about everyone needs a coach. As a part of this ClarionToolBox Series, we wanted to provide a book on coaching that:

- Can be read in an evening or weekend.
- Serves as a practical guide for getting started.
- Is easy for nonacademic people to understand.
- Brings together some of the best current thinking, research, and practice on the topic.

If you have thought about getting a coach or becoming a coach, this book is a good place to start. I draw on my experience having been coached by some of the best in the industry, having coached others for hundreds of hours over the past twenty years, and as an ICF-certified coach myself.

CURRENT THOUGHT AND PRACTICE LEADERS

Part of the value of this book is that it incorporates some of the key coaching thought and practice leaders and the hundreds of pages of their work. A few of these include:

- Richard Boyatzis, *Helping People Change*
- Henry and Karen Kimsey-House, *Co-Active Coaching*

- Pamela McLean, *The Completely Revised Handbook of Coaching*
- Michael Bungay Stanier, *The Coaching Habit*
- John Whitmore, *Coaching for Performance*
- Keith Webb, *The COACH Model for Christian Leaders*

NOTE: All these authors and titles can be found in the Reference section at the end of this book.

PPO APPROACH

In everything I teach and write, I seek to use what I call the "PPO approach." PPO refers to:

- Personal
- Professional
- Organizational

I developed this framework many years ago and honed it through my reading of "How Will You Measure Your Life?" by the late Harvard Business School professor, Clay Christensen. I recommend this work to everyone—I have all of my MBA students read the article version of Christensen's work, while my doctoral students read the full-length book by the same title. In this material, Christensen emphasizes that we do not want people who win at work but lose at life. With that in mind, my hope is that you can apply these coaching tools to your personal life as well as your professional and organizational lives.

Let's use the example of parenting. While coaching tools can be invaluable for helping your colleagues at work become more effective, I care just as much about your children as your co-workers. The journey from age 13-30 is challenging for almost every teen and young adult. As a parent, a coaching approach can work well in helping your children along this journey.

I have had many coaching clients say to me that they wish their parents had used more of a coaching approach in their relationship. I sometimes admit to them that I was not a great parent myself and that I wish I had used these tools more with my teen and adult children. Maybe you can avoid some of the mistakes I made by asking great questions and listening well to those dearest to you. You will all be better for it.

In a 2017 interview (Bariso, 2017), Microsoft CEO Satya Nadella illustrates the PPO approach as he discusses how Carol Dweck's bestselling psychology book, *Mindset*, applies to his family as well as his organization.

> I was reading it not in the context of business or work culture, but in the context of my children's education. The author describes the simple metaphor of kids at school. One of them is a 'know-it-all' and the other is a 'learn-it-all,' and the 'learn-it-all' always will do better than the other one even if the 'know-it-all' kid starts with much more innate capability. Going back to business: If that applies to boys and girls at school, I think it also applies to CEOs like me, and entire organizations, like Microsoft. (para. 3)

INTERNATIONAL COACH FEDERATION

The International Coach Federation (ICF) is the largest global certification body for professional coaches. Throughout this book we will seek to differentiate the different ways in which coaching is engaged, including:

- Informal coaching that takes place in everyday conversations.
- Formal coaching engagements that may not comply with all ICF practices and standards.

- Formal coaching practices that follow the ICF Code of Ethics and the ICF Core Competencies.

NOTE: The text of the ICF Code of Ethics and Core Competencies can be found in the appendices of this book.

INTRODUCTION

"Where do you want to go and how can I help?"

–Rick Mann

"Your advice is not as good as you think it is"

–Michael Bungay Stanier
The Coaching Habit

I have asked the question contained in the first quotation hundreds of times. To this day, when people ask to meet with me, I pose the same question. This question has many nuances that I hope you will not miss, including:

- You are probably headed somewhere.
- You probably have some hopes and aspirations for your future.
- What *you* want is most important.
- Perhaps I can be of help. If so, you will have my full attention and engagement.
- The ball is in your court, not mine.

In this introduction, I want to touch on some of the foundational principles that shape our coaching thinking and work.

DEVELOPING THE BEST VERSION OF YOURSELF

"Rick, I don't think this role is well-aligned with the best version of who you are," a good friend confided to me. I still remember the satisfaction I felt a few years later when I was in a different job that was a much better fit. Since then, I have been working with others with the goal of helping them develop the best version of themselves.

This vision of life and coaching fits with Richard Boyatzis' (2019) Intentional Change Theory (ICT). ICT focuses on developing our ideal self—a version of ourselves that addresses these questions:

- Who do I really **want to be**?
- What do I really **want to do** with my life?
- NOT: Who do others think I **ought** to be?

As coaches, our goal is to help coachees discover what their ideal self—the best version of themselves—looks like. This comes out of convictions that are rooted in a developmental growth mindset. It is imperative that we see one another as always having potential for growth and development.

GROWTH MINDSET VS. FIXED MINDSET

The growth mindset framework was largely developed by Carol Dweck (2006) at Stanford. At its core, a growth mindset believes that people can change. This contrasts with a fixed mindset, which insists that people's abilities and weaknesses are stagnant. Microsoft CEO Satya Nadella said that in 2014, Dweck's work on the growth mindset changed his life and leadership and that of Microsoft. In an interview with Jessi Hempel (2019) for LinkedIn, Nadella states:

If you take two kids at school, one of them has more innate capability but is a know-it-all. The other person has less innate capability but is a learn-it-all. The learn-it-all does better than the know-it-all. (para. 10)

In a 2014 *Inc.* article by Terence Mauri entitled "Want To Think Like Sayta Nadella? Follow 3 Simple Rules," Mauri succinctly summarizes Nadella's business approach: "the new game was to be a 'learn-it-all' company rather than a know-it-all one."

"The new game was to be a 'learn-it-all'
company rather than a know-it-all one."

A growth mindset puts more focus on effort and progress than on ability. In her key research on "grit," Angela Duckworth (2016) demonstrates that focus and discipline are greater predictors of success than talent. Our goal as coaches is to help coachees see that they can make progress in almost every area of life through attention and dedication.

KINDS OF COACHING ENGAGEMENTS

Every year, coaching seems to grow in popularity. Many think of coaching as a paid engagement between a coach and a client. In fact, there are actually several ways that coaches and coachees can work together. When I first thought about writing this book, I planned to use the word *client* instead of *coachee*. The term client is commonly understood and some wonder whether "coachee" is even a word. In my research, however, I came across one writer who reasoned that "coachee" is a better word because many coaching relationships do not involve a paid coach and paying client.

In fact, there are actually several ways that coaches and coachees can work together.

Therefore, as awkward as it may occasionally sound, I will be using "coachee" throughout this book to refer to the person who is being coached. Some of the common coach-coachee relationships include:

- Professional (paid) coaching practice
- Leader and manager as coach
- Job description coaching duties
- Coaching in an academic setting
- Volunteer coaching practice
- Parent as coach
- Group coaching

Now, let's unpack each of these arrangements. As you read through this section, remember that you may be using all of these possible options with different people.

Professional Coaching Practice

Today, the most common coaching platform is the paid professional coach. This is where a client (whom, if you will remember, we refer to as a coachee) engages a paid coach. The format usually includes one-on-one sessions in person, on the phone, or via a video call. In some cases, the client pays for these services themselves. In other cases, an organization pays for the services on behalf of the coachee.

Some professional coaches have gone through formal training programs and may be certified by a governing body like the International Coach Federation (ICF). Other coaches have developed their coaching skills on their own and practice independently.

Leader and Manager as Coach

Veteran coach Daniel Harkavy is the author of *Becoming a Coaching Leader* (2009). I still remember sitting in Daniel's Portland office years ago as we discussed how coaching could be used with college students. Since then, coaching approaches to leading and supervising have only increased. In their 2019 *Harvard Business Review* (HBR) article, "The Coach as Leader," Ibarra and Scoular observe that, "The role of the manager, in short, is becoming that of a coach" (para. 4). While coaching employees is more complicated than it sounds, today's workplace and the engagement of our workforce, particularly those of the millennial generation and younger, can benefit from a coaching approach. Ibarra and Scoular add:

> Twenty-first-century managers simply don't (and can't!) have all the right answers. To cope with this new reality, companies are **moving away from traditional command-and-control practices and toward something very different:** a model in which managers give support and guidance rather than instructions, and employees learn how to adapt to constantly changing environments in ways that unleash fresh energy, innovation, and commitment. (para. 2) [emphasis mine].

We will talk more about the coaching relationship between managers and employees in later chapters.

"The role of the manager, in short, is becoming that of a coach."

Job Description Coaching Duties

Increasingly, organizations are developing their own cadre of coaches. In these settings, coaching others is a part of a person's job description. For some, this may be just a part of their role within the company. For others, coaching constitutes the bulk of their full-time job. Some companies train their own coaches, while others outsource coaching to a third party.

Coaching in an Academic Setting

In some academic settings, teachers, professors, and staff members coach as a part of their everyday duties. Some of this may be on an informal or volunteer basis while others have coaching as a part of their formal duties. Each year, a growing number of colleges assign student success coaches to their students. Whatever they are called and however it is framed, the coach's goal in an academic setting is to see students succeed.

Volunteer Coaching

You don't have to get paid to coach others effectively. Some professionals just have a heart to see others thrive and may serve as volunteer coaches. Providing coaching services for free has both advantages and disadvantages—we will discuss those later.

Parent as Coach

As mentioned earlier, parenting teen and adult children can be a great place to apply good coaching practices. As children move from preschool to adulthood, their relationship with their parents changes. Often, adult children feel that this relationship has not changed as much as they would like. I have heard many young (and older!) adults talk about how they are weary of their parents' constant advice-giving. Nearly every teen and young adult appreciates adults around them who can ask good questions and listen well.

Nearly every teen and young adult appreciates adults around them who can ask good questions and listen well.

A coaching approach empowers your adult child to guide the relationship in a healthy way. Give some thought to how you can effectively use the coaching tools described in this book with your teen and adult children.

Group Coaching

While we tend to think of coaching as a one-on-one activity, there is also group coaching. I have designed and led group coaching activities myself and with other organizations. One format is where you take people with some common interests. You can meet together each month to discuss moving ahead on pre-selected topics or issues for each person. In another format, you meet with a functioning team and treat the whole group almost as one single coachee. There are trade-offs. While group coaching creates a different kind of confidentiality, bringing people together in a group can provide some great comradery and synergy, not to mention a reduction of time and costs.

TYPES OF COACHING

There are many types of coaching. If you read the first edition of *Co-Active Coaching* by Henry Kimsey-House, et al. and then read the fourth edition published 20 years later, you can see how much the field of coaching has expanded and diversified. In this book, I cover everything from life coaching that is appropriate for almost everyone to higher levels of leadership and executive coaching.

Life Coaching

You have probably heard of life coaching, a type of coaching that seeks to address everyday issues such as stress, health, time management, and beyond. This general form of coaching is common. While many untrained coaches start off as life coaches, some of the highest-paid coaches in the business are life coaches. Just because they are common, don't underestimate the benefits of engaging a life coach or becoming a life coach. As of 2020, I continue to meet with my life coach every month.

Health and Fitness Coaching

This coaching niche is growing every year as more and more people realize that information and education alone are insufficient to achieve the health results they want. Like so many areas of our lives and leadership, we benefit from the encouragement and accountability a coach can bring. One of the topics I bring up with my own coach each time we meet are my health and fitness goals. It makes a difference. There is some overlap between this type of coaching and a personal trainer. Some coaches and trainers in this area have specialty certifications.

Leadership Coaching

I believe that all of us can grow in our leadership. That's why I wrote *Strategic Leaders Are Made, Not Born*. A leadership coach helps people focus on those areas that can advance their leadership, regardless of whether they work in education, healthcare, business, or the nonprofit world.

Executive Coaching

At the highest levels of executive leadership, the challenges are many and complex. It is not unusual for senior leaders to feel isolated in their lives and work. A coach can provide a confidential context in which leaders can discuss the unique challenges they face. When I was a VP and CEO, I had some great coaches who gave me space and confidentiality to talk about important issues that I could not discuss with others.

As you can see, nearly everyone can benefit from coaching. Some people may want general coaching on how to be more productive as a professional. Others may want someone to talk them through choosing a new job or career or job.

OTHER TOPICS

Below, I describe a variety of other topics that come into play during formal and informal coaching engagements.

Coaching, Consulting, Mentoring, and Counseling

One of the most common questions I get about coaching concerns how coaching, consulting, mentoring, and counseling are different. In *The Completely Revised Handbook of Coaching,* Pamela McLean (2012) compares and contrasts the same four relationships using the chart below. (2012, p. 4).

	Coaching	Consulting	Counseling	Mentoring
Who receives?	Individuals Teams Organizations	Individuals Teams Organizations	Individuals Family systems	Individuals
Focus	Future focus Identifying and achieving a desired future state	Problem-solving focus Fixing a known issue and achieving greater results	Healing the past Examining repeated patterns of behaviors	Advancing in the organization Networking Understanding politics
Role of the helper	Lead from behind: client chooses the direction forward	Lead from in front: offer advice and solutions	Lead the process through questions, feedback, observations, and advice	Share past experiences as they might benefit the recipient
Helper-client relationship	Partners working together to achieve a client's stated goals	Expert (consultant) who helps the organization fix problems and grow	Expert (counselor) who helps the client	Senior, experienced individual who helps the novice
Outcomes	Goals, vision, and plan identified Forward progress on action steps	Opinions, and recommendation provided	Greater insight Healing of past	Understanding of organizational dynamics, networking
Length of relationship	Leader as coach: ongoing relationship External coach: six to twelve months to achieve significant change	Varies, depending on nature of assignment	Depends on approach of counselor; some foster ongoing relationships over years	May last over very long periods of time

While there are many ways to explain these four functions, I will try to provide a short overview of their differences. I like the definitions listed on the United States Department of Agriculture's Coaching Program website:

- **Coaching**: "The Coach's primary attention is on strengthening the client's wisdom, thought processes, and directed action toward the future, based on the client's self-identified agenda."
- **Consulting**: "A Consultant's primary attention is on helping an individual achieve personal or organizational results through the application of their specific expertise where they advise the client on the best course of action for achieving desired goals."
- **Mentoring**: "The Mentor's primary attention is on imparting wisdom to a less experienced individual by taking an active interest in their development."
- **Counseling**: "The Counselor's focus in on addressing a personal issue with a client, often related to emotions, attitude or behavior."

("Differences Between Coaching, Counseling, Managing, Mentoring, Consulting and Training," n.d., para. 2-5)

Obviously, there is a range of opinions on all of these. Don't be surprised if you find licensed counselors or psychologists emphasizing that they are the only ones in this group that are licensed. That said, even some counselors and psychologists see the overlap, as noted in Dr. Michael Bader's 2009 article in *Psychology Today*, "The Difference Between Coaching and Therapy Is Greatly Overstated." In a 2019 HBR podcast entitled "What Great Coaching Looks Like," Richard Boyatzis states:

I think an awful lot of coaching associations make a big deal out of well, if you're giving people tips, or opening doors, that's mentoring. If you're working with them about their issues, that's coaching. But if it's deep, if it's psychological then that's counseling and that's different too. And our research is showing that a lot of those differences aren't differences. (para. 15-16)

In my opinion, these four activities (coaching, consulting, mentoring, and counseling) have important differences. For example, while I have coached for hundreds of hours, I am not a licensed counselor. At the same time, I find my partnership with licensed counselors invaluable because they can address issues that I am not qualified to deal with.

Throughout this book, I talk about how we need to clearly signal these different functions. Sometimes I use the metaphor of hats to describe these transitions. If I see us moving toward a coaching function, I will ask, "Can I take a few minutes and switch from my coaching hat to my consulting hat?" If this continues, I will say, "If you would like to work through this further, it would probably be best if we did that under a separate consulting engagement."

Self-Reflection

Few coaching professionals understand the field and practices of coaching better than Pamela McLean, PhD, the founder and CEO of the Hudson Institute of Coaching. In her book, *Self as Coach, Self as Leader*, she emphasizes the centrality of self-awareness and self-reflection.

A coach simply cannot do this developmental work without first beginning at home, by thoroughly exploring, understanding, and deepening the **internal landscape of one's own self**, before proceeding to coach others. [emphasis mine] (2019, Introduction, Today's Leaders Need Coaches, para. 5)

Anyone wanting to be an effective coach needs to begin and continue down the road of growing self-awareness through self-reflection. Knowing yourself better will help you to be a better coach. For example, I have a tendency to overtalk during coaching sessions. Being aware of this allows me to employ strategies that keep the conversation focused on the coachee.

Pure Coaching vs. Blended Coaching

If you listen to many coaching experts and coaching trainers, they insist that an effective coach can coach professionals in almost any line of work. In other words, an effective coach could coach a pilot, surgeon, artist, or plumber. There is a lot of truth to this. I call this **pure coaching** because it is just a matter of skillfully engaging clients on the topics of their choice and is not related to any of the coach's own professional experience or expertise.

In Keith Webb's book, *The COACH Model for Christian Leaders*, he writes, "Take a look at these fundamental characteristics of good coaching:

- Coaches don't talk, they listen.
- Coaches don't give information, they ask questions.
- Coaches don't offer ideas; they generate ideas from clients.
- Coaches don't share their story; they tap into the client's experience.
- Coaches don't present solutions; they expand the client's thinking.
- Coaches don't give recommendations; they empower clients to choose. (2016, p. xyz)

Keith goes so far as to write, "The COACH model is pure process."

Keith is an outstanding coach and I have been fortunate to experience his excellent training. I understand what he means when he says, "Coaches don't talk, they listen." While I want to recommend Keith's book to most everyone, especially those looking for a Christian per-spective, I would say "Coaches don't talk, they listen" differently. Below, I want to discuss some of the differences between pure coaching and blended coaching.

While good coaches are versatile, we don't want to forget that good coaches have a deep understanding of themselves and the world around them. McLean (2019) speaks to this:

> The early bias assumed that "a coach is a coach" and background didn't matter because a skilled coach would be able to do great coaching with anyone. We know today this simply is not the case. Those of us coaching senior leaders need to understand organizational systems, the field of leadership, the challenges of today's world of work, and the volatile world in which we live. The old belief that a good coach can coach anyone no longer holds up. (Introduction, The Coaches They Need, para. 4)

This can be seen in the real world. Many coachees want a coach who has experience and expertise in their area of work. For some, this is because they feel such a coach can better empathize with their work. Others feel such a coach is better able to dialogue on important issues. I call this **blended or hybrid coaching.** Now, many coaching trainers will rightfully say that the role of the coach is not to train, teach, consult, or problem solve. I agree with this philosophically, but again, in real life, it is not always quite this clean and/or simple. Therefore, I will use the terms **pure** coaching and **blended** coaching throughout this book.

Coaching Sessions vs. Bringing in Coaching Tools
Much of this book will focus on effectively using tools in identified for-mal coaching sessions. This is not, however, the only way these tools can be used. There are many ways you can informally bring these tools into conversations with your friends, co-workers, and children.

For example, let's say a co-worker says to me, "Can I ask your opinion on a job I am looking at?" Having hired dozens upon dozens of people over the years, it would not be hard for me to listen and then give my opinion. However, I think bringing in a coaching approach would be more fruitful.

I could begin by asking a few questions like:

- What are you looking for in a new job?
- What strengths and weaknesses do you think you would bring to the role?
- How well does this job align with your future goals?

After some good questions and good listening, I might ask:

- How well do you think this job aligns with what you have just said?
- What might be some next steps in continuing to explore this possible job?

Bringing coaching tools into conversations keeps the focus of the conversation on the person. It helps that person to think through some of the critical issues and some possible next steps. In most cases, using coaching tools with others helps them much more than just giving them my advice. Now, let's now explore how coaching often connects with many other roles.

Coaching and Other Roles

It doesn't take very long for you to realize that coaching overlaps with other roles. We have already seen how mentoring, counseling, and consulting are similar to and different from coaching. Here is the whole list of overlapping roles used throughout this book.

1. Mentoring
2. Counseling
3. Consulting
4. Teaching
5. Training
6. Sponsoring
7. Referring
8. Resourcing
9. Supervising
10. Parenting

It doesn't take very long for you to realize that coaching overlaps with other roles.

There are times when a coaching call will have a bit of teaching or training. However, for many reasons, a coaching call is not well suited for extended teaching and training. That is when you can refer a coachee to training and teaching resources outside of the call. For example, I will sometimes discuss coachee revenue plans with them. When the conversation starts to get more technical, I might refer them to a YouTube video or book that can teach them how to use Excel to do what they need.

Below is a diagram that shows the coaching client or coachee in the middle and the activity that happens inside the coaching engagement. Sometimes, the activity moves outside the coaching engagement in a particular direction (e.g. consulting, training, etc.).

Shared Agenda

When I ask someone, "Where do you want to go and how can I help?," the focus is on their agenda. Coaching is coachee-centered, not coach-centered. That said, this doesn't mean that I am the best fit for any and everything a coachee wants to cover. I call this our shared agenda. Coachees drive the primary agenda. But I also have an agenda. I value my time and energy, and occasionally I encounter a coachee who wants to spend every session discussing their lives and work with little focus on making progress in any particular way. At some point, I will suggest that we take a break until they gain greater clarity and focus on where they want to go.

Whom Can You Coach?

Can you coach anyone? Theoretically, the answer may be yes. In real life, however, this is not exactly the case. In some circumstances, **dual relationships** (a relationship with the person other than being their coach) will come into play. Perhaps the coachee is your:

- boss or subordinate.
- relative.
- daughter's teacher.

We need to be honest with ourselves and exercise some caution on entering into coaching relationships with others that are inherently complicated. It doesn't mean that you cannot coach people with whom you have a dual relationship, just that you should do so with your full awareness. It is best to discuss potential complications before you get started.

ABCD

At the core of coaching is the belief that coachees bring many assets to the table, including their:

- Insight
- Experience
- Education
- Convictions

I like to compare this with what community development professionals call Asset-Based Community Development or ABCD. The ABCD philosophy and approach are grounded in the idea that it is better for communities to advance their work based on what they have to offer instead of what an outside agency can bring to them. In other words, the best community development happens when you start with the community's assets rather than focusing on the resources that could be brought in. For more on Asset-Based Community Development, I refer you to the website of the ABCD Institute ("ABCD Institute," n.d.) at DePaul University.

In the same way, I like to think of ABCD as Asset-Based Coaching Development. This builds on my conviction that coachees bring much to the coaching conversation. We need to focus on what the coachee brings to the conversation rather than what experience or insights the coach brings. At the end of the day, our goal is to develop independent learners and leaders who can guide and direct their own futures and are not dependent on the coach.

When I directed a Chinese language program, one of our most important goals was to develop independent learners who could resource their own learning within their communities. For example, our goal was not to teach students how to find the bus station or the bathroom. Instead, we would help them learn things like, "What is this called?" or "How would you say this?" As their independence increased, they were able to use the language they had already acquired to learn anything they needed.

Coaching Can Be Dangerous

In the June 2002 issue of *Harvard Business Review*, Steven Berglas' article entitled "The Very Real Dangers of Executive Coaching" highlights some of the problems that can arise in coaching:

- The snare of **behavioralism**: Dealing with surface-level behaviors without addressing some of the deeper issues.
- The lure of **easy answers**: When taking on the habits of a sports coach, problems ensue when coaches are quick to provide solutions for coachees.
- The **economics** of executive coaching: Some high-dollar coaching relationships are not a good investment of resources. Some inexpensive coaches are not a good value either.

- The trap of **influence**: Some coaches become powerful advisors to leaders, departing from the best practices of coaching.
- **Mental health** issues: At times, a coachee could be better served by working with a licensed mental health professional instead of a coach.

It is encouraging to see how far the coaching profession has come over the last 20 years. Are there ineffective coaches out there? Of course! However, more well-trained, effective coaches arise each year. With thoughtful awareness and effective teaching and training, most of the aforementioned problems can be avoided.

THE FIVE CS MODEL

In this section, we will review our five Cs model. Coachees lie at the center of a quality coaching engagement. The catalytic elements added to this core are good questions and good listening.

Coachee-Centered

As emphasized earlier, the core of good coaching is a coachee-centered approach. The hard work of the coach is to keep the conversation focused on the coachee.

Good Questions

If the coachee is the center of the engagement, asking good questions is crucial to the process. As a coach, nothing is more satisfying than having a coachee respond with, "That's a good question." There are many types of questions and nuances of a conversation with good questions. In later chapters, we will pull out these nuances in more detail.

Good Listening

Good listening goes well beyond hearing what someone is saying. Good listeners organize what is being said within the context of the larger conversation and use their intuition to truly understand what is being said. Good listening has these features:

- The listener is empathetic.
- The listener is attuned to body language.
- The listener connects what is said with was has already been said.

The Organic-Organized Balance

One of the tools in our broader toolbox is the organic-organized balance. In brief, the organic part of the conversation is relational, life-giving, and more fluid. On the other hand, the organized side focuses on structure, strength, and scale. Every person and organization needs the organic, life-giving side of a conversation for energy, vision, passion, and flexibility. We also need the organized side to provide strength and scale. For example, the human body is alive because the organic side is working properly. Think of this aspect as representing the organs in the body. The body has a skeleton with bones and ligaments to give it greater height and strength. You can live without properly working bones, but you won't function at your intended best.

The same principles can be applied to coaching sessions. First and foremost, coaching is organic. It is a life-giving engagement that includes vision, energy, and relational connection. The organized side of coaching includes time schedule, the stated goals, and structured next steps. Coaching is at its best when the organic/organized balance is optimized.

First and foremost, coaching is organic. It is a life-giving engagement that includes vision, energy, and relational connection.

Five Processes

Surrounding the core of good questions and good listening are the five processes that help to move the coachee forward. These five Cs include:

- Connect
- Clarify
- Collaborate
- Create
- Close

Each of these processes will be outlined in the following chapters.

PRACTICAL ISSUES BEFORE YOUR FIRST SESSION

Formal or Informal

We mentioned earlier that there are many different kinds of coaching arrangements. One of the first things to clarify is whether you are looking at a formal coaching arrangement or just an informal integration of coaching principles into an ongoing relationship. If your engagement is going to be more formal (paid or unpaid), there will be a number of things you want to clarify before you get started. Imagine someone saying to you, "Okay, let's do this coaching thing. How does it work?"

Since many people don't know how coaching works, let's look at some of the issues you will want to cover before you move forward. This can usually be done during a 30-60 minute orientation session.

Clarify How Your Sessions Will Work

You can tell your potential coachee that for typical sessions, you will meet for 30, 45, or 60 minutes every two weeks or twice a month. You can decide the length and frequency ahead of the sessions. I have seen very good professional coaches do 30-minute sessions well. Some coaches are a little more relational, but going a full-60 minutes makes the transitions to your next coachee or meeting pretty tight. This is why, like counselors, many coaches lean toward 50-minute sessions.

I usually begin by meeting with coaches every two weeks, stretching out sessions to every 3-4 weeks if needed.

What Will the First Few Sessions Cover?

There are different ways to run the first few sessions. The simplest approach is to just ask the person what they would like to address in their lives and work and go from there. Like many coaches, I like to go over an assessment in the second session. Therefore, my first session explores where they want to go and discusses how it all works. During the second session, we review a DiSC and/or MBTI assessment. The third and following sessions build from there.

Below, we will discuss getting started with a set curriculum.

Does a Series Seem to Be Developing?

When coachees want to address large topics, you may want to design a series. Here are some examples:

- Finding a new job
- Writing a book
- Processing a significant hire and onboarding

How Is Payment Going to Work?

- **Just Getting Started**: If you are new at this, I recommend that you first get a coach who can demonstrate good coaching practices for you and help you process your early coaching sessions with others. Nearly every coach benefits from a supervisor, particularly when they are new. Next, you can reach out to 3-5 family members, friends, co-workers, or others and offer to coach them at no charge. You can explain that you are training to be a coach and need to get some practice.
- **Regular Practice:** Once you have some training and practice under your belt, you can look at beginning to charge people for your coaching sessions.
- **Before or After:** Some coaches require upfront payment for a certain number of sessions or per month. Others will invoice every month or quarter after the coaching has taken place.

- **Monthly or by Sessions:** Some coaches will charge by the month, typically with a couple of sessions each month. Others will just add up the number of sessions and then invoice coachees at an agreed-upon rate.

I have done all of these arrangements and have seen others do the same. It is up to you to choose according to your preference.

Should You Use a Contract?

Some coaches regularly draw up formal contracts with coachees, while others are less formal. The ICF Code of Ethics states:

> Create an agreement/contract regarding the roles, responsibilities and rights of all parties involved with my Client(s) and Sponsor(s) prior to the commencement of services.

Your decision to use a contract depends somewhat on the nature of the coaching relationship. If you have a more formal, paid arrangement, a contract makes sense. If your coaching relationship is less formal or volunteer, the paperwork is not as important. In the Appendix, you will find a sample coaching agreement. Feel free to use this if you like, making modifications as needed.

Reviewing Confidentiality

Confidentiality is a key pillar of a coaching relationship. The coachee needs to feel certain that your conversation is not going to be shared with others. This topic can be covered more informally in conversation or more formally with a written document. Regardless, it is imperative that this trust not be broken. Here are some of the issues that can come up:

- A coachee asks you whether you are coaching Bob or Sue. You can tell them that you are not able to share that information.
- You are coaching people who know each other and they ask something about the other person. Again, you can say that you cannot share that information.

Taking Initiative

Coaches vary on how much they reach out to people for coaching opportunities. There is a sales side to a paid coaching practice which we will talk about in the Appendix.

Some coaches (like me) take responsibility for calling coachees when their scheduled session time arrives. Many other coaches leave the call-in responsibility to the coachee.

Different Time Frames: Short-Term Sessions vs. Long-Term Engagements

All five tools in this book can be applied in 30-60-minute sessions. They can also be applied to multi-month coaching engagements. Here are some examples:

Connect

- **Short-term:** Here, you are looking at the 5-10 minutes of the sessions as you get started.
- **Long-term:** This is the activity of connecting with people over the months. These small connections build on each other over time as you become more acquainted with the coachees' background, family, work, etc.

Clarify

- **Short-term:** You want to clarify your goals for this particular session as you get started.

- **Long-term:** You also want to clarify your goals for the longer engagement. This may happen once at the beginning, but it may also be updated along the way.

Collaborate
- **Short-term:** In this core section of the coaching session, you explore the topic at hand with the coachee.
- **Long-term:** In a longer and broader series, you collaborate with the coachee on a variety of topics that are relevant now, but also may be relevant in the months and years ahead.

Create
- **Short-term:** The elabloration of a plan for next steps over the coming days will be clear and specific.
- **Long-term:** The plan for the coming months and years will typically be at a higher altitude and more general. Keeping a long-term plan in view will also help keep the individual sessions on track.

Close
- **Short-term:** You want to close the session with purpose in a way that sets up the coming weeks and next call for success.
- **Long-term:** As you close off an engagement, you want the coachee to move ahead with independence and confidence. You also want to leave the door open for further sessions as needed.

In Summary

As you can see, there are many different ways you can run coaching sessions and many choices that you (and the coachee) can make. If you have a coach of your own, you may want to discuss with them how you plan on doing this in your own practice and then dialogue with them as things unfold.

1.

CONNECTING WITH CARE

*They don't care how much you know until
they know how much you care.*

"So, you're really just a paid friend?" a colleague said to me one day as we discussed coaching. I immediately realized that my colleague had never been a CEO or he would not have asked such a question. I replied by saying, "I do provide care, confidentiality, and competence to those I coach." While it is true that good friends provide these things, I have found that many senior leaders do not have friends who consistently have the time and energy to bring:

- Care
- Confidentiality
- Competence

The starting point for any good coaching relationship is trust. The coachee must have confidence that the coach genuinely cares about them. The first tool is connecting, and this must come with care.

The coachee must have confidence that the coach genuinely cares about them.

WHY IT MATTERS

A coaching relationship is a sacred trust that is founded on:

- Care
- Empathy
- Compassion

It is true that a coaching relationship can be merely transactional or that coaching can just be for compliance. However, we are looking at a coaching process that is driven by care and compassion. Richard Boyatzis, Melvin Smith, and Ellen Van Osten (2019) discuss this in their book, *Helping People Change: Coaching With Compassion for Lifelong Learning and Growth.*

> We call this coaching with compassion—that is, coaching with a genuine sense of caring and concern, focusing on the other person, providing support and encouragement, and facilitating the discovery and pursuit of that person's dreams and passions. (p. 6)

The connection you make with your coachee is the starting point for your coaching relationship.

HOW IT WORKS

Connecting with others is a combination of:

- Your mindset
- Your behaviors
- Your practices

Begin with how you frame out your coaching mindset. Why are you doing this work? Most coaches I work with are more focused on the person than the pay. Next, what are your behaviors? Do you listen well, or do you cut people off with the next thing you have to say? Proper pacing helps your coachee feel that you are listening well and engaged. Lastly, your regular practices affect your coaching relationship. Is it clear that you are interested in your coachee's life and work? Connecting is not something that happens once: it is an ongoing mindset and practice that can improve with skill development and time. Practice will help you more easily and authentically connect with your coachees.

Empathy

We all have a worldview that guides how we view and engage those around us. Some are in a hurry. Others are warm-hearted. Then there are those who just don't like being with people.

Are you an empathetic person? If so, keep it up! If not, work on your empathy skills. Empathy can be learned with practice. It begins by putting yourself in someone else's shoes and trying to see the world from their perspective. Perhaps you are a person for whom nearly everything comes quickly and easily. How do you think the person feels who finds that skill you picked up in a day difficult to learn or develop? Do you understand their frustrations and lack of confidence? If you don't, work on seeing things from their perspective.

Coachee-Focused

Rick Warren (2012) opens his well-known book, *The Purpose-Driven Life*, by saying, "It's not about you." This is a good mantra for coaches. The coach-coachee relationship is not about the coach. You may want to do some self-talking and prepare for a coaching call by repeating to yourself, "Remember, it is not about me." Your coachee should feel that you are deeply committed to their progress and success.

A simple way to assess whether your sessions are coachee-focused or coach-focused is to reflect on them and gauge what percentage of the words were spoken by the coach and the coachee. Words spoken by the coach should not exceed 50% of the session and may be as low as 25%. Make sure that the dialogue leans toward the coachee.

Connect F2F at First If You Can

As a coach, think through whether you will meet with your coachee face-to-face or use technology to see one another. There is so much more to communication than words alone. Body language can tell us a lot about what is being said. If you have a choice, it is best to start your coaching relationship face-to-face or with a video call. This way, if you end up moving to phone calls, your coachee will already feel that they have a connection with you.

Getting Their Background

As you get up and going with your coachee, it can be helpful to learn more about their background. This can include things like:

- Preferred Name
- Birthday / Anniversary Data
- Family
- Employer
- Payment Arrangements
- Why are they are interested in coaching?
- What do they hope to gain from this coaching engagement?
- Have they been in a coaching arrangement before?

You can go over this material during an early interview or you can collect this through the use of an intake form.

The Role of Assessments

Assessments can help you to more quickly understand your coachee. As of 2020, the most common assessments are:

- Myers-Briggs Type Indicator (MBTI)
- DiSC
- StrengthsFinder
- Enneagram

The International Coach Federation (ICF) website provides a review of both the MBTI and the DiSC. ICF tends to lean toward the DiSC. Here is the link: https://coachfederation.org/blog/disc-vs-mbti-assessments.

Their review emphasizes that the MBTI is more inward-focused while the DiSC is more work focused. In my university work, we have historically used the MBTI more. I use the DiSC more in my coaching work.

"Assessments are helpful, but not perfect."

Why use an assessment? They help the coach and the coachee to get to know each other more quickly and can also help the coachee grow in self-awareness. I typically go over a person's DiSC assessment during our second session.

If you want to coach others regularly, I suggest that you take all four of these assessments for yourself, become fluent in two of them, and use one of them in your work. Note that there are some free versions of some of these. With students, I often use a free version of the MBTI found at: www.16personalities.com.

In summary, remember that "assessments are helpful, but not perfect." They provide space to talk about personality and work. Even when a coachee finds an assessment section that is not a good fit, it provides space for a conversation to discuss this further.

Should You Use a Curriculum or Not?

Some coachees will start off with a basic curriculum. Daniel Harkavy's coaching group, Building Champions, starts off with a LifePlan that coaches and coachees work through together. In the first few sessions, I will often use my book, *Strategic Leaders Are Made, Not Born: The First Five Tools for Escaping the Tactical Tsunami*. In using this book with coachees, I like to focus on:

- **Creating Value:** What do you provide that others value?
- **Developing Self-Awareness:** How are you unique?
- **Analyzing Stakeholder Relationships:** Whom do you serve?
- **Elevating Your Strategic Altitude:** At what altitude do you lead?

At a minimum, I usually discuss their goals in the first session and go over the DiSC in the second session. By that point, I understand them better and we have established some trust. I use the DiSC assessment and some of the material from *Strategic Leaders Are Made, Not Born* to give us some common understanding. You do not have to start with an assessment or curriculum to coach well. You can begin by learning what your coachees want to focus on and go from there.

WHAT TO DO NEXT

The first thing you want to do with your coachees is connect. In an informal coaching arrangement, spend time together asking good questions and listening well to get to know the person better. With a more formal coaching engagement, begin by exploring with the coachee what brings them to this point, what they hope to gain from their time with you, and how coaching sessions normally work.

Connecting in Each Session

Connecting happens in every coaching session. The goal is to connect effectively with care and compassion. Here are some practical ways you can connect during your coaching session.

Before you connect with your coachee, prepare yourself by:

- Getting ready and settled in heart, mind, and soul.
- Focusing on the person with whom you will be connecting.
- Reviewing your notes from the last session so you can recall how things ended with purpose in your last session.
- "Leaning into" the coming sessions with focus and emotion.

Start With a Warm Greeting

All of us enjoy connecting with warm-hearted people that bring authentic engagement, greetings, and connections. When you are coaching in-person, show that you care with a smile and appropriate body language. Depending on your context and culture, that first contact could be a handshake. Avoid being too cold or too embracing. Like Goldilocks and the Three Bears, you want your physical connection and presence to be just right.

If you are on a video call, you can demonstrate your connection with your body language as well. If you are on a phone, you have to communicate your warmth through your voice. Regardless, as the coach, you want to bring some energy to your opening connection.

Open With Some Important, But Simple Questions

I will sometimes ask, "Bob, since we talked last, what is new in your world?" Ask your coachees to catch you up on what has happened since your last session. Look at your notes and bring up something that has been happening in their lives. You can also ask them about their health, work, family, etc. You don't want to jump right into a topic if they had a death in the family last week.

Reviewing Action Steps From the Last Session

As you review your notes from your last session, look at the topics and issues discussed as well as the specific next steps that were affirmed. Ask the coachee about the agreed-upon action items from your last session. We will talk more about taking notes in later sections.

Celebrate the Wins

As the coachee shares their progress, be affirming. Even if their progress seems small, join with them in celebrating their wins. Be aware of yourself as to whether things come easy for you or whether you need some practice. Make sure not to interject with your own accomplishments. The focus should be on the coachee and their wins.

If You Are New at Coaching, Practice

It may take you a while to get comfortable connecting with others. Thoughtfully practice making connections so that you can feel comfortable as well as authentic doing so. After the session is over, reflect back on the connecting that happened at the start of the session.

After 5-10 Minutes, Move On

While connecting at the beginning of a session is so important for a good start, be careful not to get sidetracked. If you have a 50-60-minute session, you can take 15 minutes here. If your session is only 30 minutes, you will need to keep things moving after 5-8 minutes. Connect relationally and emotionally, then follow-up by transitioning to the next phase: Clarifying the Path Forward.

Connecting Long-Term

As you connect with your coachee during each session, you are building a valuable understanding of their world. Keep some notes on their:

- Family
- Work
- Future plans
- Financial goals
- Health and fitness

When I was living in Minnesota, I had a great family physician. After a year of not seeing him, I came in for my annual physical. In passing, he asked me about the progress of our son's graduate school studies. When I got home, I told my wife, Cheri (a nurse practitioner), how amazing it was that he could remember those details about my life. She looked at me and said, "Rick, he writes it down." I should have known.

Just like that physician, we can keep notes on our coachees' lives to help us stay connected with them on their journey. Whether you choose to record notes on paper or digitally, most of us have too many coachees to keep track of every detail they share with us in our heads.

2.

CLARIFYING THE GOAL

*"When you don't know where you are going,
any road will get you there."*

–Lewis Carroll
Alice in Wonderland

"What would be most helpful in this session?" is a common question of mine. Once you have connected with your coachee, you are ready to explore the direction of the session. Coaching sessions work better when you have clarity on where the coachee wants to go.

WHY IT MATTERS

Coaching sessions that are focused are more productive than those that wander. The best sessions flow out of clarity on the part of the coachee as to where the session needs to go. The coach can help the coachee clarify and confirm the direction and goals of the session. When coachees struggle to clarify their desired path forward, the coaching process can suffer as well. Thankfully, as you will learn in the following sections, there are some things you can do if issues arise.

HOW IT WORKS

Keep the following principles in mind as you and your coachee decide how to move forward. First, and foremost, we want to keep things in the hands of the coachee. While coaches can help facilitate the exploration of this direction, they should not be the ones who decide. Second, sessions should be focused so that the right amount of material can be covered in a single session. When the focus is too broad for a single session, you can address the issues in a series of several sessions.

Where Does the Coachee Want to Focus?

In each chapter of this book, we want to reaffirm the principle that control and direction ultimately lie with the coachee, not the coach. Suppose the coachee is not initially clear on the direction they want to go in. Through good questions, good listening, and collaboration, the coach can help the coachee settle on an appropriate focus for the session.

Coaching Back

Sometimes a coachee will want to work on applying material they have already read. This coach-back strategy can work well when the coach uses the session to help the coachee integrate the recently-read material into their life and work. For example, perhaps they recently read an article about time management, dealing with crises, or writing a blog and want to see how they might apply these concepts to their personal and professional lives. As mentioned in the introduction, coaching sessions are not well-suited for teaching extended concepts or material. I would recommend that the coachee:

- Work through the material before the session.
- Briefly summarize the key concepts.
- Explore how the they can put the material to use in the coming weeks and months.
- Create a plan forward so they can track their progress.

Some coaches use this coach back strategy with set materials as a starting point for moving forward. The following books are some that are well-suited for the coach back strategy.

- *Strategic Leaders Are Made, Not Born* by Rick Mann (2019)
- *The Seven Habits of Highly Effective People* by Stephen Covey (1989)
- *Traction* by Gino Wickman (2012)
- *Becoming a Coaching Leader* by Daniel Harkavy (2010)
- *Leading Change* by John Kotter (2012)
- *The Advantage* by Patrick Lencioni (2012)

Narrowing the Focal Point of the Session

Some coachees will want to discuss broader and higher-level topics such as:

- I want to change jobs
- I want to write a book.
- I want to retire.

When the coachee introduces these sizeable topics, it can be helpful to break them into a multi-session series. In the series, you can address a smaller piece of the puzzle in a single session. For example, if the coachee wanted to discuss getting a new job, you could design each session around one of the questions below:

- What is working and not working in your current job?
- What are some of your long-term hopes vocationally?
- What is the market like for the job you want?
- What are your needs financially, time-wise, and physically?
- Are you open to going back to school to move this forward?
- What is your process and timeline for this?

I Have Nothing Today, Can We…?

When a coaching session gets started, you will find people in all kinds of conditions. Some coachees are settled, focused, and ready to go. Others are stressed by the world around them. Lastly, you will have a few people who don't have the focus or energy for a session. Once you have connected with your coachee, you can take a few minutes to assess where to go next. Here are a few options.

- **Regular Session**: Most of the time, you will have some previous clarity on your direction, and you can simply move forward.
- **Regathering Yourself:** Sometimes, the coachee may be distracted by a recent event. Maybe their child is in the hospital; they have lost their job; or some other event has left them unable to pick up from the last session. In these cases, the coach can re-focus on the need of the hour—as outlined by the coachee—and have a very productive session nonetheless.
- **Tool Session**: Occasionally, a coachee will say that they do not have the focus or energy to move the session forward. They will sometimes ask me if we can do a tool session. During a tool session, we cover a particular tool they want to learn and talk about how to apply it their lives and work. For example, we could discus time tracking as a strategy for greater productivity. Generally, coaching sessions are not well-designed for teaching and training. There are times, however, when that is the preferred direction of the coachee.
- **Reschedule**: When a session is not able to go forward as scheduled, it may be best to reschedule. Your coaching agreement will guide whether a rescheduled session comes with a cost or not.

What To Do Next

In this segment of the coaching session, the goal is to take 10 minutes or less to clarify the path forward for this session. When I ask, "What would be most helpful in this session?", coachees often reply with sufficient clarity and we can move on. I usually restate the goals that the coachee has expressed to make sure that they are clear for both of us. When you work with a coachee, remember to listen well, restating what they have said back to them to ensure both parties are tracking well.

Clarifying Each Session

Some coaches will review the focus of the next session so they can more quickly move to that focus at the next session. Some will even go so far as emailing the coachee a day or two ahead as a reminder.

There is a balance here. You don't want to be so organized that you miss fruitful work on issues that have come up recently. This is where it is important to realize that each coachee is different. Some coachees are very structured and move ahead with clarity and focus session after session. Others are more spontaneous and will have issues that come up that they want to discuss.

When a coachee has a front burner issue that has just come up that they want to focus on, it is fine to move away from the structured agenda to deal with these topics. If new "front-burner" issues arise at nearly every session, you should voice your concern that perhaps things are too chaotic.

Clarifying Long-Term

While it is helpful to clarify the goals for individual sessions, it is also important to continue clarifying the goals of your overall coaching engagement, which may cover several months. For example, you could talk about how the coachee is working toward becoming a better public speaker. Five months from now, you may want to update that goal or move on to another long-term goal in a different direction.

NOTE: Occasionally, some coachees struggle with clarity and progress session after session. In this situation, I suggest pausing coaching sessions for the time being and picking them up at a later date when the coachee feels they have more clarity on where to go or what to work on.

3.

COLLABORATING CREATIVELY

WITH QUESTIONS

Good questions are more important
than good answers.

Coaching is about a partnership between the coach and coachee to maximize the coachee's forward progress. Once we have established the coachee as the center of the conversation, the coach can collaborate with the coachee in exploring the topics at hand. This coaching section, which is usually the longest, uses questions to probe and develop the coachee's thinking.

WHY IT MATTERS

When working together, two heads are better than one. The coach can help the coachee clarify where they want to go and then explore how to get there. The best coaching relationships are collaborative, working synergistically to advance the coachee's goals. When a conversation is one-sided, it is typically less productive. If a coach talks too much during a session, the value to the coachee is decreased. If the coachee talks the whole time, the necessary reflection may be neglected. A happy medium is reached when the coach asks the right questions in the right way in order to foster the coachee's constructive thinking.

HOW IT WORKS

The discussion at this point is where the coach and coachee are actively engaged in the topic of the session. As mentioned earlier, the coach must be mindful not to dominate the conversation.

It Is Not About Telling (Chronic Tellers)

Many capable and experienced leaders are Chronic Tellers. When I was a new consultant, I once visited a client along with the founder and principle of the consulting firm. As we were leaving a session with the senior team, the president of the organization stopped my colleague and told her, "Hey, I am retiring soon and would love to work with your firm."

Afterwards, I asked my colleague how often this happened to her. She told me it happened all the time. I then asked her why she hired me instead of them because they were much more famous in their industry. She replied, "All they want to do is stand in front of people and tell them all the things they have done. People want someone who will bring expertise, ask good questions and listen well." In other words, people do not want to hire Chronic Tellers as coaches or consultants.

Many capable and experienced leaders
are Chronic Tellers.

As Michael Bungay Stanier writes in his book, *The Coaching Habit: Say Less, Ask More, and Change the Way You Lead Forever:*

Tame the Advice Monster
Tell less and ask more.
Your advice is not as good
As you think it is. (p. 59)

Good Coaching Is About Good Listening

At the heart of good coaching is the habit and skill of good listening. Good listening begins with active engagement through giving the person your full attention and focus. From the outside, it may look like the coach is doing nothing, but in fact, the coach is totally focused on the coachee's:

- words
- body language
- tone of voice
- emotions

At the heart of good coaching is the habit and skill of good listening.

Empathy

Instead of thinking about what the coach is going to say next, the coach can use empathy to enter into the thoughts and words of the coachee. Empathetic listening is a challenging and learned skill. It begins with managing your own thoughts and emotions so that you can focus on the person. Empathy requires stepping into someone else's shoes so you can see and feel things from their perspective. On the importance of empathy to good coaching, Annie McKee writes in her 2016 HBR article, "If You Can't Empathize with Your Employees, You'd Better Learn To":

Empathy—the ability to read and understand other's emotions, needs, and thoughts—is one of the core competencies of emotional intelligence and a critical leadership skill. It is what allows us to influence, inspire, and help people achieve their dreams and goals. Empathy enables us to connect with others in a real and meaningful way, which in turn makes us happier and more effective at work.

Pamela McLean (2012) also stresses the importance of empathy. In her book, *The Completely Revised Handbook of Coaching*, she cites Empathetic Stance as one of the key domains and capacities:

> The coach's ability to experience and convey empathy is a pivotal element in this work. One's capacity to walk in the shoes of another and experience the feelings of another defines empathy. It doesn't require a lot of words, but it does necessitate that we notice the feeling state of another and convey that we see him or her in this state and are at home in this space with the client. (p. 25).

Collaborating effectively with your coachee means empathetically connecting with their thoughts and emotions. With this foundation, the coach is at a better place to ask better questions.

Good Questions Are at the Heart of Good Coaching

Good coaching practices connect good questions with good listening. An engaged and skilled coach will consistently hear the coachee saying, "Good question!" It is about asking the right kind of questions at the right time for this particular coachee. This process may sound simple, but it is magic when it happens well. Let's look at the variety of questions that are available to coaches.

Different Kinds of Questions

Just as an experienced craftsman has a variety of tools in their toolbox, a good coach needs a number of different kinds of questions in their repertoire. Here are some simple, starting types.

- **Factual Questions**: Factual questions are often used to begin conversations. Some examples could be "How long have you been at this job?" or "Where did you go to college?" These are easy questions to get things up and going. This is not to say that these questions are not helpful. Factual questions are used every day to help you get better acquainted with your coachee in a way that is not abrupt for them.
- **Feeling Questions**: Once you are acquainted with where your coachee is at today, you can delve deeper with feeling questions. Going deeper in a conversation and in a relationship is an important part of the journey. Examples of feeling questions could be "How do you feel about your current work?" or "How do you feel about your co-workers?" Notice how fact and feeling questions can be paired together. You could ask, "What is your current role at your company?" and then follow up with "How are you feeling about this role?"
- **Reflection Questions:** The most challenging and perhaps most strategic questions are reflection questions. For example, you could ask, "When you think back on the past five years in your current role, what would you have done differently?" or "Where would you like to be in five years?"

Much has been written on using questions in coaching. I recommend looking at Tony Stoltzfus' (2008) book, *Coaching Questions: A Coach's Guide to Powerful Asking Skills*. In this 100-page book, you will find hundreds of helpful questions to use in your sessions.

Open-Ended and Closed Questions

Closed questions can be answered in a single word or simple phrase—questions like "Are you happy with your job?" or "Are you going to move to Denver?" Such closed questions usually do not usually create the rich results we are looking for. As Lena Katz (2020) writes on this topic:

> For stronger connections, better insights, and more business, experts recommend one conversational tool above all in the demo or discovery phase: open-ended questions. (para. 2)

Open-ended questions foster deeper thinking and reflection for the coachee. Here are some examples of open-ended questions:

- What would you do differently next time?
- What do you think a person would need to do to be successful in this job?
- What are some ways that you could address your procrastination?

Coaching conversations benefit from a wide variety of questions. The goal is to foster thoughtful processes in the coachee's mind, resulting in high ownership for their steps leading forward.

Questions and Brain Research

The latest brain research helps us to realize that different kinds of questions affect the brain differently. Boyatzis, et. al write:

> we begin to focus on how to build resonant relationships and learn to ask the right questions of one another—while listening to the answers—to evoke learning and change. **Both style and timing of questions can inspire the PEA** [Positive Emotional Attractor] and change, or the opposite. Missing key moments and getting questions out of sequence can turn a

possibly motivating conversation into a guilt-inducing grilling. (Emphasis mine)

A coach who asks thought-provoking questions ("What do you see in your drawing?" "What's important to you in your life?") can awaken a person's PEA, activating parts of the brain that trigger hormones—the parasympathetic nervous system (PNS)—that is associated with emotions such as **awe, joy, gratitude, and curiosity.** (Emphasis mine) (p. 155)

It Is About the Coachee

While we have discussed the importance of a coachee-centered approach at several points throughout this book, it is beneficial to mention it here as well. When you think of asking good questions, remember that the purpose of the process is to foster the coachee's self-discovery. If the coach asks questions only out of their own curiosity, it may not serve the coachee well. Keep focusing on questions that are best suited to advancing the coachee's development.

WHAT TO DO NEXT

As you practice your coaching skills, consider recording some of your sessions so that you can go back and listen to the questions you asked. Once you have listened to the questions in your session, reflect on the quantity, quality, and type of questions you have used.

Consider whether you are using the appropriate mix of factual, feeling and reflective questions. Some coaches keep a list of questions in front of them, particularly when they are on a remote call.

Take some time to expand your repertoire of questions so that you don't become repetitive. For example, I like to start off sessions with "What is new in your world?" After a few times, this can get redundant, so I expand that to "Has anything come up since our last session?" or "What has been most pressing for you in recent days?" You can grow your list of questions or consult any one of the coaching books listed at the end of this book.

Collaborating in Each Session

During each session, the collaboration section offers an opportunity to help the coachee develop their own insights and steps forward. Before the session starts and as it proceeds, think about which questions would be best for the situation at hand.

Collaborating Long-Term

As you move from session to session, you may find yourself needing fewer factual questions and more reflective questions to help the conversations go deeper.

Also, as time goes on, you can occasionally ask some summary questions. Here are some examples:

- As we review our last 3-4 sessions, how are you doing with the pacing of our sessions?
- What have we covered that you have found most helpful?
- As we look forward, how are we doing on covering the key topics you wanted to address?

4.

CREATING A PLAN FORWARD

"Life is like riding a bicycle, to keep your balance, you must keep moving."

–Albert Einstein

"If you can't fly then run, if you can't run then walk, if you can't walk then crawl, but whatever you do you have to keep moving forward."

–Martin Luther King, Jr.

The goal of every coaching relationship is to support the coachee's goals moving forward. Before a coaching session ends, it is important to spend some time clarifying the next steps.

WHY IT MATTERS

If you don't clarify the next steps, coachees will not maximize the benefits of the session. It is easier than you think to have great conversations only to have little clarity at the end and make little progress over time. When next steps are lacking, there can be a loss of momentum.

HOW IT WORKS

Once your conversation has adequately covered the collaborative phase, you are ready to create a plan forward. As coach, it is your responsibility to manage the time during the coaching session. When there are at least 5-10 minutes left in the session, you should shift to Creating a Plan Forward.

It Starts With Them

This part of the coaching session is not about telling the coachee what to do next. Rather, the focus is on exploring what would be most helpful in moving the coachee forward. You want to ensure that they have ownership of what they are going to do next.

It is easy to say what you think the coachee needs. A coach I was training once asked me, "Rick, it is clear to me what this person needs. Why not just tell them and be done with it?"

There are many reasons not to tell coachees what to do next. First, the coachee is the one who is going to take these next steps, thus it is critical that the ownership lies with them. Second, the coach does not know the coachee's context as well as the coachee does. Issues of time, relationships, competing agendas, etc. can affect the coachee's ability to address next steps.

If next steps were just about information, most people would stop smoking or lose weight. As we know, there are many factors that come into play when people consider what they will do or won't do. Moving forward means putting actions to our goals.

Be SMART

Many of us are familiar with SMART goals. SMART goals share these features:

- Specific
- Measurable
- Attainable
- Realistic
- Time-Based

These features can help your coachee take hold of practical goals that are going to move them forward.

Say a coachee wants help managing stress. The coach might ask them, "What would be some helpful next steps to move forward?"

The coachee responds, "I should get some more exercise this week."

The coach could reply with, "Can you give me some more detail on what that exercise might look like this week?"

"Sure. I will run three days this week for at least 30 minutes," the coachee answers.

This is quite good. The only think you might ask at some point is how fast they plan to run. This short interchange takes the general goal of exercising more and adds the what, when, where, and how. The more specific the next steps are, the more likely it is that the coachee will move forward.

In her popular 2012 book, *Nine Things Successful People Do Differently*, Heidi Grant Halvorson lists "Getting Specific" first. She writes:

> Being specific about what you want is just the first step. Next, you need to get specific about the obstacles that lie in the way of getting what you want. In fact, what you really need to do is go back and forth, thinking about the success you want to achieve and the steps it will take to get there. This strategy is called mental contrasting, and it is a remarkably effective way to set goals and strengthen your commitment. (p. 8)

When you help coachees get specific about their next steps, their chances of progress are improved.

Focus on Progress, Not Perfection

In advancing their goals and taking the next steps, coachees don't need to get it all right every time. They should feel your support more than the need to get it perfect. Follow-up will happen during the Connect portion of the next coaching session. Encourage the coachee to write down their next steps and then mention that you will touch base on them in your next session.

One-Foot Fence

With many coaching sessions, especially those that are more informal, I use the principle of the **one-foot fence** (thanks to Don Larsen for this helpful tool). A one-foot fence is something that is very attainable with some attention and effort.

Here are some examples of one-foot fences:

- Walk for 10 minutes.
- Set an appointment date with a counselor.
- Log their exercise time for the week.

A one-foot fence is purposely easy to attain. In most cases, it is not an issue of time or effort. Instead, it is an issue of willingness. Usually, if the person is willing, they can get some easy and early wins. If a coachee consistently neglects one-foot fences, it may be an issue of focus, desire, and discipline.

I explore one-foot fences with coachees during most sessions. They are very helpful in allowing me to understand the coachee's level of engagement with the coaching process. If the coachee rarely engages even simple one-foot fences, that tells me that they have low interest in the coaching process or struggle with execution. Most coachees will follow through at some level. If the coachee follows through on every one-foot fence, it tells me they are very eager and may mean that we need to raise the challenge or increase the pace of the coaching process.

Set a Follow-Up Process

Clarify what you hear your coachee saying with them. For example, you might say, "So, what I hear you saying is that before our next session, you would like to …" Affirm their direction and commitment by mentioning that you will follow-up with them on these issues at the beginning of the next session.

If, during the follow-up, the coachee doesn't remember the next steps, you may want to ask the coachee how they normally track action steps in their daily life and work. Some coachees will need coaching in this important area because they struggle with organization and follow-through.

Some coaches-in-training will ask whether they should write down the next steps and send a reminder to the coachee. Generally, this is not a good habit because we are working toward the coachee being independent in their own future development. I will usually write down the next steps for my own reference, but I don't send them to the coachee.

WHAT TO DO NEXT

About ten minutes before a session concludes, you can ask, "What next steps would help you to make progress on the things we have discussed today?"

If a coachee struggles with this, you can provide 2-3 examples. Remember, don't tell them they should do A or B. When you do this, it takes the ownership from them and transfers it to you—something that needs to be avoided.

Keep It Realistic

If the coachee is very ambitious and says they want to run a marathon this Saturday and they haven't trained, you may want to push back just a bit and suggest that they break down that ambitious goal into smaller pieces over a longer time frame.

Creating in Each Session

During a session, there are a number of great opportunities to create next steps that can be transformational for the coachee over the coming days. You can also raise the altitude of planning and look at the next steps over the coming years. While most of the conversations in this phase will be short-term and session-oriented, don't miss out on opportunities to look at the wider horizon.

Creating Long-Term Next Steps

When a coachee suggests large-scale next steps, it is a good time to discuss breaking those steps into smaller pieces that can be covered over several sessions. For example, if the coachee says they would like to take their spouse on an overseas trip, the coach can explore the several steps needed with the coachee. Picking dates, exploring locations, planning the itinerary, etc. will need to be addressed. The coach and coachee may need a number of weeks and sessions to pull all this together.

Summary

The Creating a Plan Forward phase is not the longest segment of a coaching session, but it may be the most strategic. Helping the coachee take ownership over their goals and next steps can lead to the transformational progress the coachee desires. Over the years, I have seen many examples of how a coachee's life and work are transformed.

For some coachees, transformation happens through the content area they are addressing as they reach their new goals. For example, maybe they are working on fitness goals and making progress. For others, the process of goal setting and execution is transformational in itself. Many coachees have not had much success at setting goals and seeing them reached through practical action steps. Practicing this skill in different areas can help them develop newfound independence to advance what they care about.

5.

CLOSING WITH PURPOSE

*"Often when you think you're at the end
of something, you're at the beginning
of something else."*

–Fred Rogers

"What was most helpful in our session today?" I asked my coachee.

"I am very encouraged with the clarity gained in this session and how I can now see some practical steps forward." they replied.

As a coach, nothing is more rewarding that hearing a response like that at the end of a session. Finishing a session well can help to maintain the momentum of the coaching dynamic going forward.

WHY IT MATTERS

Closing out a session with purpose provides an ongoing sense of progress and momentum that can carry the coachee forward. Sometimes the closing can be the most important five minutes of the whole session. The closing also provides an opportunity to affirm the coachee and their desire to learn and grow. When a session ends abruptly, it can cause the coachee to wander over the coming days.

HOW IT WORKS

The closing allows the coach and coachee to look back over the session and review all that has been covered. I closed a recent coaching call by doing the following:

- **Connecting**: We talked about the coachee's recent travels and their visit with their family as well as the progress they had made since our last call.
- **Clarifying**: We discussed how we had accomplished the goals of our sessions.
- **Collaborating**: We were able to cover two major topics, including some field research they wanted to do and some videos they wanted to develop. The coachee mentioned how the verbal processing of these two topics was helpful.
- **Creating**: We were able to create next steps for these two topics and plan how we would touch on them in our next session.
- **Closing**: I asked if there was anything they wanted to discuss that we didn't have time for during this session. The coachee said they wanted to discuss some issues related to team dynamics.

All these areas were touched on during the last five minutes of our session. These short minutes allowed us the opportunity to review and reinforce all that we had covered.

Reviewing the Next Steps

A few questions or restatements that can help cement a good plan going forward include:

- So, what do you see as the next steps coming out of this session?
- So what I hear you saying is that your next steps are…
- It sounds like your 2-3 one-foot fences going forward are…

The goal here is to have the coachee take ownership of their steps forward. You can help your coachee with this by talking about where they are going to keep track of their next steps. For example, they could write them down in a notebook or make a list on their phone.

Writing It Down

In the last chapter, we discussed the fourth segment of the Five Cs model— creating a plan going forward. Creating a plan is not enough. The next step is leaning into implementation. A good step in this direction is to write it down in a notebook or calendar.

Social psychologist Heidi Grant Halverson (2011, p. 173), describes an experiment in which people were invited to complete a certain task by a certain date. Those who wrote down the specific plan were more than TWICE as likely (71%) to complete the task than those who didn't (32%). In her 2012 book, *Nine Things Successful People Do Differently*, she insists, "To seize the moment, decide when and where you will take each action you want to take, in advance. Again, be as specific as possible" (pp. 15-16).

As you close, ask your coachee what works best for them when it comes to keeping track of things they need to do. If they have no system in place or struggle to accomplish things, you may need to address this topic in a later session.

Those who wrote down a specific plan were more than TWICE as likely (71%) to complete the task.

Closing a Session With Follow-Up to Follow

As your coachee clarifies their next steps, you can mention that you will touch base with them on this as you connect in your next session. Providing this accountability and follow-up will help the coachee maintain focus on their agreed-upon next steps.

Scheduling the Next Session

Normally, with adults, I like to schedule sessions about two weeks apart. Some professional coaches with many coachees schedule sessions out many months ahead by giving them a certain time slot, such as every other Tuesday at 10am. For many people this works well. I am not one of them. I am an ENTP on the MBTI and have many moving pieces in my life. Therefore, **at the end of each session, I schedule the next session.** This works well for coaches and coachees who have a schedule that changes from week to week.

Closing a Series or Coaching Engagement

You may wonder how a coaching engagement ends. First, it is good to recognize that the majority of coaching engagements are for months, not years. Here are some ways to wrap up a coaching engagement.

- **Start with a set number of sessions**: You can start with 3-5 sessions if you want and then renew them if both parties agree.
- **Cover a certain topic or series:** Maybe your coachee wants coaching on getting a new job. Once they land that job, you can wrap things up.
- **The engagement is losing momentum.** After you have coached someone for several months, you may notice that their engagement and energy are beginning to wane. At this point, I ask them if we have accomplished their goals or if they still have more they want to cover.

- **There is a consistent lack of progress.** Some coachees will eventually struggle to move ahead on their one-foot fences. If this happens, I will suggest that maybe they are too busy and offer to pause our sessions. I then invite them to re-engage the process at a later date if they wish.

WHAT TO DO NEXT

As you lead sessions, assess how well you are managing to Close With Purpose. If things seem too vague, you may want to add a bit more clarity and structure to your closings. Remember that no two coachees are the same. They may want or need different styles. Some Christian coachees like to close sessions with prayer. Others do not. The goal here is to learn about your practices and tendencies and then develop the ability to adapt as needed.

Closing Each Session
As mentioned above, closing a session involves reviewing what has been covered as well as future commitments. Next, you will want to schedule the next session on your calendars. Lastly, you can affirm the coachee and the progress they are making.

Long-Term Coachees
I am one of those long-term coachees. I have met with my coach every month for the last several years and plan to continue to do so every month for the next several years. Why do I continue this ongoing coaching engagement? For one simple reason: it continues to bring much more value than cost in helping me to be the best version of myself. Also, I believe that coaches are best when they have some kind of supervision. Not only do I talk about my own issues and goals with my coach every month, I will also use some of our sessions to confidentially debrief on my time with my coachees.

In summary, most coaching relationships will last for months. However, I have been coached for years, and at times, I have had some coachees for years.

Closing in the Long Term

As you have repeated coaching sessions with the same coachee, keep your head and heart open for when the time seems best to enter the off-ramp for the coaching engagement. The closing may not be this session, but it may come up a few sessions down the road. Sometimes I ask coachees about where they are in their own journey of independence. If the timing seems right for the off-ramp, there are a few things you will want to do before you are finished.

- **Finalize payments.** If you have any outstanding payments that are due, clarify those arrangements with your coachee.
- **Network development.** Encourage your coachee to develop a network of personal and professional contacts they can use in the months ahead for support and encouragement in continued growth.
- **Stay in touch.** You can decide whether you want to stay in touch or not. Some coaches and coachees will stay in touch over the coming months and years.
- **Starting again in the future.** Sometimes, coachees will circle back in later months or years as they have issues that come up in their lives and work.

CONCLUSION

We have now covered the Five Cs framework in some detail. If you are new at this, the next steps are to get a coach yourself and then to begin practicing in real sessions. Even if you are a veteran coach, there are still things to learn.

---

*Coaching is a journey for both the coach
and the coachee.*

As you will see, coaching is a journey for both the coach and the coachee. There are always new insights to be gained about ourselves as coaches and the wide variety of coachees with differing personalities and needs. Keep learning and keep investing in yourself and others.

APPENDIX A:
GETTING STARTED

If you have not done much coaching before, here are some practical ways to get started. In this section, we suggest how you can apply these coaching tools to a wide variety of relationships. If you don't think that you can get started with coaching, you may want to watch a YouTube video by the Box of Crayons guy, Michael Bungay-Stanier, entitled "The Guide to Effective Coaching in 10 Minutes." Michael has a lot to say about coaching and this video is very good.

Getting a Coach
The best place to start is by finding a coach for yourself. Working with a coach will hopefully allow you to experience good coaching practices firsthand. This relationship may also provide some supervision and/or support for your own coaching journey.

Peer Coaching
If you have a friend or colleague who is also interested in coaching, you can set up a peer coaching engagement. This arrangement often works well in conjunction with this book or other shared training. Boyatzis (2019) writes, "Peer coaching formalizes a personal, supportive connection for mutual help" (p. 157). You and your peer coach could plan weekly coaching sessions, alternating who serves as coach and who serves as

the coachee. You can learn a lot in just three months' time because you will have coached for six sessions and been coached for six sessions.

Practice With a Friend, Family Member, or Colleague

I suggest that you read through this book, find a coach, and get started coaching others.

Reach out to a friend, co-worker, or family member and tell them you are looking to get some coaching experience for free. Start with 5-10-20 sessions that are 30-45 minutes in length and that are in-person, on a video call like Zoom for FaceTime, or on the phone.

Getting Formal Training as a Coach

Formal training will provide you with an in-depth engagement of the best coaching principles and practices. There are dozens of programs out there to choose from. If you want some suggestions, you can contact us at info@clarionstrategy.com.

When you think about revenue from coaching, you might want to build out a 4x5 that can model this for you. For more detail on 4x5s, read our ClarionStrategy book, *Strategic Finance for Strategic Leaders,* by Rick Mann and David Tarrant (2020). This process will help you to think through your assumptions, resulting revenue, expenses, and net income.

Individual Coaching Practice Example

		FY1		FY2		FY3		FY4		FY5
Assumptions (Price/Volume)										
Coaching Clients		10		15		20		30		40
Coaching Sessions/Month		2		2		2		2		2
Coaching Session Rate	$	75.00	$	100.00	$	125.00	$	150.00	$	150.00
Coaching Payment/Session	$	50.00	$	75.00	$	100.00	$	125.00	$	125.00
Income										
Coaching Revenue	$	18,000.00	$	36,000.00	$	60,000.00	$	108,000.00	$	144,000.00
Total Revenue	$	18,000.00	$	36,000.00	$	60,000.00	$	108,000.00	$	144,000.00
Expense										
Coach Payment	$	12,000.00	$	27,000.00	$	48,000.00	$	90,000.00	$	120,000.00
Website	$	1,000.00	$	2,000.00	$	3,000.00	$	4,000.00	$	5,000.00
Marketing	$	1,000.00	$	2,000.00	$	4,000.00	$	6,000.00	$	8,000.00
Other expenses										
Total Expenses	$	14,000.00	$	31,000.00	$	55,000.00	$	100,000.00	$	133,000.00
Income from Operations										
Income from Operations (EBIT)	$	4,000.00	$	5,000.00	$	5,000.00	$	8,000.00	$	11,000.00
Other Expenses										
Interest	$	-	$	-	$	-	$	-	$	-
Income Before Taxes	$	4,000.00	$	5,000.00	$	5,000.00	$	8,000.00	$	11,000.00
Income Taxes 30%	$	1,200.00	$	1,500.00	$	1,500.00	$	2,400.00	$	3,300.00
Net Income/Metrics										
Net Income from Operations	$	2,800.00	$	3,500.00	$	3,500.00	$	5,600.00	$	7,700.00

APPENDIX B:

RELATED COACHING ROLES

Coaching is an activity that touches on a number of different domains. For example, let's say you are coaching a client and you begin to touch on some content issues. You can certainly incorporate a bit of teaching in a session, but for several reasons, doing extended teaching during a coaching session is not the best for the client. First, teaching is not at the heart of the coaching process. Second, it is inefficient and expensive. While it may be appropriate to touch on these different domains within a coaching session, at some point, a domain becomes too prominent and the coach needs to either change hats or refer the client to a different session or person.

The most common areas of overlap with coaching include:

- Mentoring
- Counseling
- Consulting
- Teaching
- Training
- Sponsoring
- Referring
- Resourcing
- Supervising
- Parenting

Mentoring

Mentoring is one of the most common areas of overlap with coaching. By "mentors," we are describing those who care and are supportive. Mentors who are often older than then their mentees usually share their experiences in conversation.

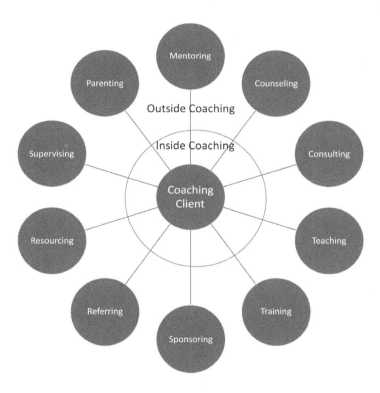

Coaches also care and are supportive. The key difference between mentoring and coaching is that in coaching, the focus is on the coachee's goals and experience. Also, most coaches have training and/or certification in coaching.

Mentoring is often less focused and structured than coaching. Further, a mentor relationship may go on for months or years and is usually not a paid role. On the difference between mentoring and coaching, McLean (2012) writes in *The Completely Revised Handbook of Coaching*:

> The earliest notion of coaching was closely linked to the concept of mentoring. In our first edition of this book, we used the term mentor-coaching and wrote: Mentoring is the model for coaching . . . but the word mentor is too formal for purposes of a coach training model. I prefer the term coach here. Coach is now applied to a person who facilitates experiential learning that results in future-oriented abilities. This term (coach) refers to a trusted role model, adviser, wise person, friend, mensch, steward or guide—a person who works with emerging human and organizational forces to tap new energy and purpose, to shape new visions and plans, and to generate desired results. A coach is someone trained and devoted to guiding others into increased competence, commitment and confidence. (p. 6)

> Experience reveals a good deal about the important distinctions and overlaps among the disciplines of coaching, mentoring, consulting, and advising. **Mentoring was a natural bridge to coaching, but it offers a limited view of the domain of coaching** and the essential elements of the field. Understanding important differences between coaching and mentoring and the distinctions and overlaps relative to the fields of consulting and coaching provides role and boundary clarity for today's coach. (p. 3) [Emphasis mine]

NOTE: In my experience, mentoring often works better than coaching for those under 25 years of age because many younger adults are looking for support more than structured progress.

Counseling

Coaching and counseling have significant similarities and differences. A key similarity is that both are client-centered. Their objective is to empower and support clients in reaching their goals. One key difference is that licensed counselors are mental health professionals, while coaches are not.

As a coach, I find that counselors are critical partners to my coaching practice. For example, say I am talking with a coachee about some trouble they are having at work. After some listening and discussion, I suggest that the client see a licensed counselor on this because the conversation has gone past my ability address the needs they have.

In some cases, I continue coaching a client even as they meet with a counselor. In other cases, I suggest that they work through their issues with a counselor and then come back if they want to continue.

Consulting

I typically think of coaching as something I do with individuals and teams to help them get better at what they do, while consulting looks at the organization as a larger system. They are both important, but they are not the same. I find McLean's (2012) characterization of coaching as leading from behind while consulting is leading from the front (p. 4) particularly appropriate.

In a coaching session, the client may bring up some organizational consulting. We can discuss these in the context of their coaching goals. If it gets more involved, I will recommend that we move this discussion out of our coaching session to a consulting session or to a consulting engagement with someone else.

Since I do both coaching and consulting work, I am sometimes asked whether I typically start with coaching and then move to consulting. I have done it both ways. Sometimes when I am coaching a leader, they will invite me to consult on issues related to their larger organization. At other times, I am doing a consulting work with the organization on their issues and a leader or team will ask if I can do coaching with them.

Teaching

Coaching is not the best modality for teaching content. Sometimes there is a place to share content with your client. That said, I will often resource the client with materials they can engage outside of the coaching session. At times, we will then cycle back to the topic to discuss application.

To take one example, I discuss the concept of strategic altitude with many of my coaching clients. I can resource them on this topic by referring them to Chapter 4 of my short book, *Strategic Leaders Are Made, Not Born*. We can then come back to the concept and discuss how strategic altitude might move them forward in their goals.

Training

If teaching is about knowledge and understanding, training is about skill development. Let's say that a coachee mentions that they want to improve their writing or public speaking. I would not spend much time in the coaching session to go over this kind of training. Instead, I would point them to material they could use for this area. We could then return to the topic later and look at how they desire to move forward.

Sponsoring

Many clients have professional goals that may involve new roles in different organizations. For example, maybe a staff accountant wants to become a controller but that is not available at their organization. At times, the coach may have connections with people and organizations that could help the client moving forward. This sponsoring function can be invaluable in helping your coachee reach their goals.

Referring

An important role of the coach is referring clients to others. This happens when the coach realizes that others can serve the client better than the coach. I often refer clients to counseling or to another leader or mentor. I will also refer clients to other coaches whose specialty is a better fit for their goals than mine. I tend to focus more on leadership coaching than on life coaching, so if a coachee wants to get help in that area, I'll refer them to a colleague.

Resourcing

There is an infinite world of resources out there on an endless number of topics. This includes YouTube, podcasts, courses, degree programs, training opportunities, books, journals, and so forth. It is often appropriate for the coach to point clients in the direction of these materials.

Supervising

Daniel Harkavy (2010) was one of the earlier voices on the coach as supervisor with his book, *Becoming a Coaching Leader* (2010). These days, you hear more and more discussion around the supervisor as coach.

It is important here to briefly mention the concept of dual relationships. This refers to the fact that at times, we are connected to people in more than way. For example, if I were an elementary school principal and my daughter was in the third grade at the school, her third-grade teacher would have one relationship with me as the principal and a second relationship with me as the father of one of his third-grade students. Our dual relationship is not unworkable, but it does complicate things. In the same way, when a supervisor coaches an employee, there are at least two things going on. First, the supervisor needs to move the organization forward. Second, the supervisor is seeking to help the employee grow and develop. A coaching supervisor can be a wonderful step forward in supporting and developing employees.

In this situation, I recommend to supervisors that they pick a different time and perhaps even a different location for coaching sessions. For example, you might meet with your direct report in your office on Tuesday mornings to discuss work, while on Thursday afternoons, you could meet at the corner coffee shop to discuss the person's professional development. Also, in a meeting with the direct report, the agenda is directed by the supervisor. In a coaching meeting, the agenda should be shaped by the employee, not the supervisor.

Supporting

Coaches want to support clients and see them make progress. Many senior leaders, especially CEOs can face significant isolation or even loneliness. In such situations, the coach's support can be invaluable. At times, however, some coachees will move sessions that focus more on support and less on progress. This is fine unless it becomes chronic and on-going. If I find a client is mostly looking for support in our sessions rather than focusing on making progress, I talk with them about their broader support network.

Like all these roles, supporting the coachee is an important dimension of any coaching session. If it becomes the primary focus, it might be best to move this function outside of your coaching sessions.

Parenting

Yes, parents can serve as coaches to their children. One of my personal and professional passions is helping teens and young adults on their journeys from age 13 to age 30. Asking good questions and listening well can be invaluable gifts for your teen or young adult.

Like the role of supervisor as coach, coaching teens is a dual relationship that involves both the supervision of a minor and the development of a young adult. As your children move through their twenties, it is more about development and less about supervision.

Rather than using formal coaching sessions with your children, I would encourage you to just integrate these five tools into your everyday conversations and relationship.

APPENDIX C:

EXAMPLE COACHING

AGREEMENT

Coach's Name: _____

Coachee's Name: _____

The purpose of this coaching agreement is to help clarify expectations for this coaching engagement. Here are the provisions outlined in this agreement.

- Coaching sessions are strictly confidential and will not be shared with others unless authorized in writing by the coachee.
- Authorized person: _____
- Once payment for sessions has been completed, I realize that this coaching agreement may be discontinued at any time.
- Payment will be provided BEFORE / AFTER (choose one) coaching sessions are provided.
- Payment will be made by the SESSION / MONTH (choose one) at a rate of _____ until this date: _____.

- Coaching sessions will usually be conducted via PHONE / via VIDEO/ or IN-PERSON (Choose one).
- Once scheduled, coaching sessions will rarely (1 out of 10) be cancelled or changed.

Coachee's Signature: _____ Date: _____

Coach's Signature: _____ Date: _____

APPENDIX D:

ICF CERTIFICATION

You may want to pursue additional training and possible certification by the International Coach Federation (ICF). While ICF is not the only group that provides certification for coaching, ICF is the largest global certification body for professional coaches.

ICF is the largest global certification body for professional coaches.

WHY ICF CERTIFICATION?

There are many programs that offer certified coaching training. Why would you want to have ICF coaching certification? In a coaching industry that is very unregulated, ICF certification is the gold standard. It tells the public that you have meet the rigorous standards of the leading global certification body. ICF partners with professional training programs to ensure that programs meet the following:

Certified Professional Coach training is a 60-hour ICF approved and accredited coach training program. Participants undergo extensive coaching skills learning through various classroom learning methodologies and fieldwork to build on elementary level coaching skills and get certified as a professional coach at level 1. In addition to 60 hours of coach training, participants also undergo 10 hours required mentor coaching in 2 sessions of 3.5 hours of group mentoring & 3 sessions of 1 hour each one on one mentoring. (ICF website)

Training Programs

There are many coaching training programs out there that are accredited by the ICF and can lead to ICF certification.

As you look at ICF-certified coaching training programs, there are several factors to consider.

- Focus and Culture
- Modality
- Cost
- Location
- Time Frame

NOTE: I began my ICF certification training many years ago with the International Coach Academy. I then restarted the process by doing coaching certification training through Keith Webb's Creative Results Management Coaching Mastery Certificate Program. I then followed this up with the additional ICF-required work (e.g. 100 hours of coaching sessions where I coached others) to finally meet all the ICF certification requirements.

Focus and Culture

Each coaching program has a unique focus and culture. Some focus on life coaching, while others focus on leadership coaching. Some focus on women or men. Some are in English and have a U.S. focus. Others are in English or another language and have an international or non-U.S. focus.

Modality
Some training programs are done entirely in-person, while others are entirely online or via phone. Some are blended in modality.

Cost
Coaching certification training usually runs more than $1,000 and less than $10,000.

Location
Coaching training is available online and in many countries (usually in larger cities).

Time Frame
ICF-certification coaching training can be completed in just a week intensive (with follow-up), over some months, or even over more than a year. Make sure to not confuse ICF-approved training with full ICF certification training.

NOTE: You may be able to take ICF-approved training in a week intensive or over a month or two, but ICF certification takes much longer because you have to do at least 100 post-training hours of coaching with others.

ICF-Approved or Not
Some training programs are ICF-approved and some are not. You can find other training that is certified by an organization (e.g. John Maxwell) or other international bodies such as the International Coaching Association (ICA).

ICF CERTIFICATION PROCESS

Getting your ICF certification is a multi-stage process that includes:

- ICF-approved training program.
- Coaching others for at least 100 documented hours after your training has been completed (including some paid hours).
- Submitting a recording and transcript of a coaching session.
- Passing the ICF test.

CONTINUING EDUCATION

Once you have obtained ICF certification, you will need to undergo continuing education to maintain that certification. You must complete at least 40 hours of Continuing Coaching Education coursework every three years.

ICF CODE OF ETHICS

The ICF Code of Ethics is Composed of Five Main Parts:

1. Introduction
2. Key Definitions
3. ICF Core Values and Ethical Principles
4. Ethical Standards
5. Pledge

1. INTRODUCTION

The ICF Code of Ethics describes the core values of the International Coach Federation (ICF Core Values), and ethical principles and ethical standards of behavior for all ICF Professionals (see definitions). Meeting these ICF ethical standards of behavior is the first of the ICF core coaching competencies (ICF Core Competencies). That is *"Demonstrates ethical practice: understands and consistently applies coaching ethics and standards."*

The ICF Code of Ethics serves to uphold the integrity of ICF and the global coaching profession by:

- Setting standards of conduct consistent with ICF core values and ethical principles.
- Guiding ethical reflection, education, and decision-making
- Adjudicating and preserving ICF coach standards through the ICF Ethical Conduct Review (ECR) process
- Providing the basis for ICF ethics training in ICF-accredited programs

The ICF Code of Ethics applies when ICF Professionals represent themselves as such, in any kind of coaching-related interaction. This is regardless of whether a coaching Relationship (see definitions) has been established. This Code articulates the ethical obligations of ICF Professionals who are acting in their different roles as coach, coach supervisor, mentor coach, trainer or student coach-in-training, or serving in an ICF Leadership role, as well as Support Personnel (see definitions).

Although the Ethical Conduct Review (ECR) process is only applicable to ICF Professionals, as is the Pledge, the ICF Staff are also committed to ethical conduct and the Core Values and Ethical Principles that underpin this ICF code of ethics.

The challenge of working ethically means that members will inevitably encounter situations that require responses to unexpected issues, resolution of dilemmas and solutions to problems. This Code of Ethics is intended to assist those persons subject to the Code by directing them to the variety of ethical factors that may need to be taken into consideration and helping to identify alternative ways of approaching ethical behavior.

ICF Professionals who accept the Code of Ethics strive to be ethical, even when doing so involves making difficult decisions or acting courageously.

2. KEY DEFINITIONS

- "Client"—the individual or team/group being coached, the coach being mentored or supervised, or the coach or the student coach being trained.
- "Coaching"- partnering with Clients in a thought-provoking and creative process that inspires them to maximize their personal and professional potential.
- "Coaching Relationship"—a relationship that is established by the ICF Professional and the Client(s)/Sponsor(s) under an agreement or a contract that defines the responsibilities and expectations of each party.
- "Code"—ICF Code of Ethics
- "Confidentiality"—protection of any information obtained around the coaching engagement unless consent to release is given.
- "Conflict of Interest"—a situation in which an ICF Professional is involved in multiple interests where serving one interest could work against or be in conflict with another. This could be financial, personal or otherwise.
- "Equality"—a situation in which all people experience inclusion, access to resources and opportunity, regardless of their race, ethnicity, national origin, color, gender,

sexual orientation, gender identity, age, religion, immigration status, mental or physical disability, and other areas of human difference.

- "ICF Professional"—individuals who represent themselves as an ICF Member or ICF Credential-holder, in roles including but not limited to Coach, Coach Supervisor, Mentor Coach, Coach Trainer, and Student of Coaching
- "ICF Staff"— the ICF support personnel who are contracted by the managing company that provides professional management and administrative services on behalf of ICF.
- "Internal Coach"— an individual who is employed within an organization and coaches either part-time or full-time the employees of that organization.
- "Sponsor"—the entity (including its representatives) paying for and/or arranging or defining the coaching services to be provided.
- "Support Personnel"—the people who work for ICF Professionals in support of their Clients.
- "Systemic equality"—gender equality, race equality and other forms of equality that are institutionalized in the ethics, core values, policies, structures, and cultures of communities, organizations, nations and society.

3. ICF CORE VALUES AND ETHICAL PRINCIPLES

The ICF Code of Ethics is based on the ICF Core Values (link) and the actions that flow from them. All values are equally important and support one another. These values are aspirational and should be used as a way to understand and interpret the standards. All ICF Professionals are expected to showcase and propagate these Values in all their interactions.

4. ETHICAL STANDARDS

The following ethical standards are applied to the professional activities of ICF Professionals:

SECTION I – RESPONSIBILITY TO CLIENTS

As an ICF Professional, I:

- Explain and ensure that, prior to or at the initial meeting, my coaching Client(s) and Sponsor(s) understand the nature and potential value of coaching, the nature and limits of confidentiality, financial arrangements, and any other terms of the coaching agreement.
- Create an agreement/contract regarding the roles, responsibilities and rights of all parties involved with my Client(s) and Sponsor(s) prior to the commencement of services.
- Maintain the strictest levels of confidentiality with all parties as agreed upon. I am aware of and agree to comply with all applicable laws that pertain to personal data and communications.
- Have a clear understanding about how information is exchanged among all parties involved during all coaching interactions.
- Have a clear understanding with both Clients and Sponsors or interested parties about the conditions under which information will not be kept confidential (e.g., illegal activity, if required by law, pursuant to valid court order or subpoena; imminent or likely risk of danger to self or to others; etc.). Where I reasonably believe one of the above circumstances is applicable, I may need to inform appropriate authorities.

- When working as an Internal Coach, manage conflicts of interest or potential conflicts of interest with my coaching Clients and Sponsor(s) through coaching agreement(s) and ongoing dialogue. This should include addressing organizational roles, responsibilities, relationships, records, confidentiality and other reporting requirements.

- Maintain, store and dispose of any records, including electronic files and communications, created during my professional interactions in a manner that promotes confidentiality, security and privacy and complies with any applicable laws and agreements. Furthermore, I seek to make proper use of emerging and growing technological developments that are being used in coaching services (technology- assisted coaching services) and be aware how various ethical standards apply to them.

- Remain alert to indications that there might be a shift in the value received from the coaching relationship. If so, make a change in the relationship or encourage the Client(s)/Sponsor(s) to seek another coach, seek another professional or use a different resource.

- Respect all parties' right to terminate the coaching relationship at any point for any reason during the coaching process subject to the provisions of the agreement.

- Am sensitive to the implications of having multiple contracts and relationships with the same Client(s) and Sponsor(s) at the same time in order to avoid conflict of interest situations.

- Am aware of and actively manage any power or status difference between the Client and me that may be caused by cultural, relational, psychological or contextual issues.

- Disclose to my Clients the potential receipt of compensation, and other benefits I may receive for referring my Clients to third parties.

- Assure consistent quality of coaching regardless of the amount or form of agreed compensation in any relationship.

SECTION II – RESPONSIBILITY TO PRACTICE AND PERFORMANCE

As an ICF Professional, I:

- Adhere to the ICF Code of Ethics in all my interactions. When I become aware of a possible breach of the Code by myself or I recognize unethical behavior in another ICF Professional, I respectfully raise the matter with those involved. If this does not resolve the matter, I refer it to a formal authority (e.g., ICF Global) for resolution.
- Require adherence to the ICF Code of Ethics by all Support Personnel.
- Commit to excellence through continued personal, professional and ethical development.
- Recognize my personal limitations or circumstances that may impair, conflict with or interfere with my coaching performance or my professional coaching relationships. I will reach out for support to determine the action to be taken and, if necessary, promptly seek relevant professional guidance. This may include suspending or terminating my coaching relationship(s).
- Resolve any conflict of interest or potential conflict of interest by working through the issue with relevant parties, seeking professional assistance, or suspending temporarily or ending the professional relationship.
- Maintain the privacy of ICF Members and use the ICF Member contact information (email addresses, telephone numbers, and so on) only as authorized by ICF or the ICF Member.

SECTION III – RESPONSIBILITY TO PROFES-SIONALISM

As an ICF Professional, I:
- Identify accurately my coaching qualifications, my level of coaching competency, expertise, experience, training, certifications and ICF Credentials.
- Make verbal and written statements that are true and accurate about what I offer as an ICF Professional, what is offered by ICF, the coaching profession, and the potential value of coaching.
- Communicate and create awareness with those who need to be informed of the ethical responsibilities established by this Code.
- Hold responsibility for being aware of and setting clear, appropriate and culturally sensitive boundaries that govern interactions, physical or otherwise.
- Do not participate in any sexual or romantic engagement with Client(s) or Sponsor(s). I will be ever mindful of the level of intimacy appropriate for the relationship. I take the appropriate action to address the issue or cancel the engagement.

SECTION IV – RESPONSIBILITY TO SOCIETY

As an ICF Professional, I:
- Avoid discrimination by maintaining fairness and equality in all activities and operations, while respecting local rules and cultural practices. This includes, but is not limited to, discrimination on the basis of age, race, gender expression, ethnicity, sexual orientation, religion, national origin, disability or military status.

- Recognize and honor the contributions and intellectual property of others, only claiming ownership of my own material. I understand that a breach of this standard may subject me to legal remedy by a third party.
- Am honest and work within recognized scientific standards, applicable subject guidelines and boundaries of my competence when conducting and reporting research.
- Am aware of my and my clients' impact on society. I adhere to the philosophy of "doing good," versus "avoiding bad."

5. THE PLEDGE OF ETHICS OF THE ICF PROFESSIONAL:

As an ICF Professional, in accordance with the Standards of the ICF Code of Ethics, I acknowledge and agree to fulfill my ethical and legal obligations to my coaching Client(s), Sponsor(s), colleagues and to the public at large.

If I breach any part of the ICF Code of Ethics, I agree that the ICF in its sole discretion may hold me accountable for so doing. I further agree that my accountability to the ICF for any breach may include sanctions, such as mandatory additional coach training or other education or loss of my ICF Membership and/or my ICF Credentials.

For more information on the Ethical Conduct Review Process including the links to file a complaint, please click the button below.

Adopted by the ICF Global Board of Directors September 2019 © 2020 International Coach Federation

ICF COMPETENCY MODEL FOUNDATION

Demonstrates Ethical Practice

Definition: Understands and consistently applies coaching ethics and standards of coaching

- Demonstrates personal integrity and honesty in interactions with clients, sponsors and relevant stakeholders
- Is sensitive to clients' identity, environment, experiences, values and beliefs
- Uses language appropriate and respectful to clients, sponsors and relevant stakeholders
- Abides by the ICF Code of Ethics and upholds the Core Values
- Maintains confidentiality with client information per stakeholder agreements and pertinent laws
- Maintains the distinctions between coaching, consulting, psychotherapy and other support professions
- Refers clients to other support professionals, as appropriate

Embodies a Coaching Mindset

Definition: Develops and maintains a mindset that is open, curious, flexible and client-centered

- Acknowledges that clients are responsible for their own choices
- Engages in ongoing learning and development as a coach
- Develops an ongoing reflective practice to enhance one's coaching
- Remains aware of and open to the influence of context and culture on self and others
- Uses awareness of self and one's intuition to benefit clients
- Develops and maintains the ability to regulate one's emotions
- Mentally and emotionally prepares for sessions
- Seeks help from outside sources when necessary

CO-CREATING THE RELATIONSHIP

Establishes and Maintains Agreements

Definition: Partners with the client and relevant stakeholders to create clear agreements about the coaching relationship, process, plans and goals. Establishes agreements for the overall coaching engagement as well as those for each coaching session.

- Explains what coaching is and is not and describes the process to the client and relevant stakeholders
- Reaches agreement about what is and is not appropriate in the relationship, what is and is not being offered, and the responsibilities of the client and relevant stakeholders
- Reaches agreement about the guidelines and specific parameters of the coaching relationship such as logistics, fees, scheduling, duration, termination, confidentiality and inclusion of others
- Partners with the client and relevant stakeholders to establish an overall coaching plan and goals
- Partners with the client to determine client-coach compatibility
- Partners with the client to identify or reconfirm what they want to accomplish in the session
- Partners with the client to define what the client believes they need to address or resolve to achieve what they want to accomplish in the session
- Partners with the client to define or reconfirm measures of success for what the client wants to accomplish in the coaching engagement or individual session
- Partners with the client to manage the time and focus of the session
- Continues coaching in the direction of the client's desired outcome unless the client indicates otherwise

- Partners with the client to end the coaching relationship in a way that honors the experience

Cultivates Trust and Safety

Definition: Partners with the client to create a safe, supportive environment that allows the client to share freely. Maintains a relationship of mutual respect and trust.

- Seeks to understand the client within their context which may include their identity, environment, experiences, values and beliefs
- Demonstrates respect for the client's identity, perceptions, style and language and adapts one's coaching to the client
- Acknowledges and respects the client's unique talents, insights and work in the coaching process
- Shows support, empathy and concern for the client
- Acknowledges and supports the client's expression of feelings, perceptions, concerns, beliefs and suggestions
- Demonstrates openness and transparency as a way to display vulnerability and build trust with the client

Maintains Presence

Definition: Is fully conscious and present with the client, employing a style that is open, flexible, grounded and confident

- Remains focused, observant, empathetic and responsive to the client
- Demonstrates curiosity during the coaching process
- Manages one's emotions to stay present with the client
- Demonstrates confidence in working with strong client emotions during the coaching process
- Is comfortable working in a space of not knowing
- Creates or allows space for silence, pause or reflection

COMMUNICATING EFFECTIVELY

Listens Actively

Definition: Focuses on what the client is and is not saying to fully understand what is being communicated in the context of the client systems and to support client self-expression

- Considers the client's context, identity, environment, experiences, values and beliefs to enhance understanding of what the client is communicating
- Reflects or summarizes what the client communicated to ensure clarity and understanding
- Recognizes and inquires when there is more to what the client is communicating
- Notices, acknowledges and explores the client's emotions, energy shifts, non-verbal cues or other behaviors
- Integrates the client's words, tone of voice and body language to determine the full meaning of what is being communicated
- Notices trends in the client's behaviors and emotions across sessions to discern themes and patterns

Evokes Awareness

Definition: Facilitates client insight and learning by using tools and techniques such as powerful questioning, silence, metaphor or analogy

- Considers client experience when deciding what might be most useful
- Challenges the client as a way to evoke awareness or insight
- Asks questions about the client, such as their way of thinking, values, needs, wants and beliefs
- Asks questions that help the client explore beyond current thinking

- Invites the client to share more about their experience in the moment
- Notices what is working to enhance client progress
- Adjusts the coaching approach in response to the client's needs
- Helps the client identify factors that influence current and future patterns of behavior, thinking or emotion
- Invites the client to generate ideas about how they can move forward and what they are willing or able to do
- Supports the client in reframing perspectives
- Shares observations, insights and feelings, without attachment, that have the potential to create new learning for the client

CULTIVATING LEARNING AND GROWTH

Facilitates Client Growth

Definition: Partners with the client to transform learning and insight into action. Promotes client autonomy in the coaching process.

- Works with the client to integrate new awareness, insight or learning into their worldview and behaviors
- Partners with the client to design goals, actions and accountability measures that integrate and expand new learning
- Acknowledges and supports client autonomy in the design of goals, actions and methods of accountability
- Supports the client in identifying potential results or learning from identified action steps
- Invites the client to consider how to move forward, including resources, support and potential barriers
- Partners with the client to summarize learning and insight within or between sessions

- Celebrates the client's progress and successes
- Partners with the client to close the session

APPENDIX E:

COACHING SYSTEMS

Sometimes a leader will call wanting to be coached. At other times, a leader calls because they want to develop coaching systems within their organization. The latter is a more complicated systems issue with many factors that come into play. We will address a number of these issues in this section.

Increasingly, companies are developing a coaching culture. Thought leader Richard Boyatzis (2019) speaks to this trend:

> Creating an effective coaching culture requires a range of management skills and thoughtful discernment—everything from assessing overall need and managing access to coaches, to (sometimes) centralizing coach training and certification to ensure quality. (p. 156)

Boyatzis goes on to discuss the particular importance of coaching for women and underrepresented minorities:

> They (two researchers) noted that women remain underrepresented in leadership roles and are underpaid as a group. Coaching therefore could provide professional women with a safe place to contend with issues like career advancement in male-dominated fields and to reflect on work-life integration. (p. 155)

Creating an effective coaching culture requires a range of management skills and thoughtful discernment.

4 TIERS OF COACHING

I suggest we look at a coaching system from a 4-tiered perspective:

- Coachee
- Coach
- Coaching Supervisor
- Head Coach

Let's look at each of these levels to see the dynamics that are involved.

COACHEE

Many organizations want to provide coaching resources for their employees. This will often come with some resources for coaching. One of the first issues is whether these resources come from inside or outside the organization.

Internal vs. External Resources

Internal resources can be provided by training coaches within the organization and then engaging them with employees. Another option is to provide funding for employees to engage external coaches. Both internal and external approaches have advantages and disadvantages.

Internal coaches know the organization, the structures, and the culture. This can be very helpful for employees as they seek to navigate their professional development. The downside of internal coaches is that some feel that the level of confidentiality is not as high. Also, it can be awkward for the employee to change coaches if things are not going well.

External coaches can bring greater objectivity and confidentiality to the process but they lack an understanding of the organization and may be more expensive.

Each organization has to decide whether it wants to train internal coaches, engage external coaches, or have a mix of both.

Voluntary or Required

Another question for organizations to answer is whether specific roles will be coached or whether the opportunity will be optional. I encourage organizations to provide coaching as a voluntary opportunity. Requiring coaching can reduce the empowerment that is at the center of coaching.

Remedial Coaching

Sometimes, organizations will assign a coach to an underperforming employee. In my experience, if coaching is required, it often does not go well. A better choice is to make an external coach available to employees. They can then decide whether they want to access that coaching or not.

COACH

Given that this entire book is about coaching, not much needs to be said here. Every coach should be aware of the internal/external and voluntary/required dynamics. In addition, I believe it is ideal for all coaches to have a person who provides them with supervision and/or support.

For example, an organization could have a trained coach on their staff. The coach could engage coachees as well as being supervised by a coaching supervisor from inside or outside the organization.

COACHING SUPERVISOR

Ideally, every coach has someone to interact with as a coach, mentor, or supervisor. This provides for ongoing accountability, mental health, and professional growth.

Support

Coaches can become isolated if they regularly coach people one-on-one. In the midst of this journey, coaches can benefit greatly from the support of a coaching supervisor. As the coaching process can be emotionally draining for the coach, a supportive supervisor can provide some restoration for the soul.

> *Ideally, every coach has someone to interact with as a coach, mentor, or supervisor.*

Accountability

Sometimes coaches get themselves into difficult spots where they may have some ethical issues arise. This can happen through the natural processes of transference and countertransference. A coaching supervisor can help coaches avoid difficult and even harmful situations.

Mental Health

Coaching and counseling can take a toll on the heart and soul of the coach and counselor. When coaches have clients that are particularly difficult, the supervisor can help the coach address these issues in healthy ways.

Professional Growth

Growing coaches have ongoing strategies for personal and professional growth. The best coaches participate in self-reflection with themselves and others. Additionally, there are a wealth of resources that can help in the growth of the coach. A supervisor can help the coach's growth journey.

Head Coach(es)

The head coach is the person who is often responsible for the whole coaching system within a system or organization. This person can be an employee of the organization or an outside consultant. Either way, you are ideally looking for a leader who:

- Has been coached.
- Has successfully coached others.
- Has been through coaching training.
- Has vision and passion for the transforming work that coaching can bring to the lives and leadership of others.
- Is able to provide ongoing leadership for at least 2-3 years.

WHAT SHOULD OUR ORGANIZATION DO NEXT?

There are several next steps to consider:

- Talk to a consultant or two about how this could look for your organization.
- See if you can talk with others in other organizations that have developed coaching systems within their organizations.
- Talk with your leaders to see if you have a sustaining vision and culture that could successfully develop a sustained coaching culture.
- Begin by coaching some of your leaders for 3-6 months to see how things develop within your organization.

Developing a Coaching Culture

Organizations have a growing desire to develop a coaching culture. In a 2018 Forbes article entitled, "What Does a Coaching Culture Look like?", Tracy Cocivera writes:

> In fact, **a strong coaching culture correlates positively with higher employee engagement** and financial performance, specifically revenues above that of industry peers.
>
> If you ask people working in a strong coaching culture, they'll also tell you the indicators that show it's working include:
>
> - Improved team functioning: 57%
> - Increased employee engagement: 56%
> - Increased productivity: 51%
> - Improved employee relations: 45%
> - Faster leadership development: 36%
>
> There are **three primary modalities** to utilize when creating a coaching culture: external coaches, internal coaches and managers/leaders using coaching skills. Those who have found the greatest benefit are those who know which one to unleash at what time. Sixty-four percent of organizations with existing strong coaching cultures use all three modalities, while only 33% of other organizations do. (para. 9)

Richard Boyatzis and his colleagues (2019) outline three ways to develop a coaching culture.

> As these examples illustrate, creating an effective coaching culture requires a range of management skills and thoughtful discernment—everything from assessing overall need and managing access to coaches, to (sometimes) centralizing coach

training and certification to ensure quality. We also see in these examples three basic approaches to offering coaching services in organizations: (1) encourage and train associates to peer coach in pairs or teams; (2) provide access to internal or external coaches (people professionally trained as coaches and typically certified by some professional group); and/or (3) educate and develop managers and senior leaders to provide coaching to their direct reports and others. (p.156)

Advancing Women and Minorities

Coaching has been proven to advance the careers of women and minorities.

> In one of our many discussions with Miggy and Deb, they noted that women remain underrepresented in leadership roles and are underpaid as a group. Coaching therefore could provide professional women with a safe place to contend with issues like career advancement in male-dominated fields and to reflect on work-life integration. They also found that researchers recommend coaching for helping both women and minorities find their unique voice and advance through organizational structures. You can see how similar dynamics might also be present in our families and communities. (p. 155)

Moving Forward

Consider how coaching might advance your organization can advance the mission and effectiveness of your organization. You could begin by reading this book with a few colleagues and discussing how coaching might be used to develop your people.

RECOMMENDED READING

Foundational Articles

"Why You Should Develop a Coaching Culture Within Your Organization" by Austin Baker (2019). HR Professionals Magazine. https://hrprofessionalsmagazine.com/2019/06/14/why-you-should-develop-a-coaching-culture-within-your-organization/

"Two Types of Business Coaching" by Dave Busse (2017). EssentialImpact.com. https://essentialimpact.com/blog/the-two-types-of-business-coaching/

"The Leader as Coach" (2019). Herminia Ibarra and Anne Scoular. https://hbr.org/2019/11/the-leader-as-coach

"How Great Coaches Ask, Listen, and Empathize" by Ed Batista (2015). *Harvard Business Review.* https://hbr.org/2015/02/how-great-coaches-ask-listen-and-empathize

Foundational Books

Co-Active Coaching (Third Edition) by Henry Kimsey-House, Karen Kimsey-House and Phillip Sandahl (2011),
This is an early coaching bible.

Strategic Leaders Are Made Not Born by Rick Mann (2019).
Foundational material for creating value for those around you.

Helping People Change by Richard Boyatzis, Melvin Smith, and Ellen Van Oosten (2019).
Introduction to compassionate coaching.

Coaching Questions by Tony Stoltzfus (2008).
A treasure chest of useful questions for most every coach.

The Coach Model for Christian Leaders by Keith Webb (2019).

A standard for those coaching in a Christian setting.

Advanced Books

The Completely Revised Handbook of Coaching: A Developmental Approach (Second edition) by Pamela McLean (2012).

A comprehensive overview of almost all relevant coaching topics.

Self as Coach, Self as leader by Pamela McLean (2019).

An in-depth look at how the inner workings of a coach's personality affects their coaching work.

REFERENCES

ABCD Institute. (n.d.). Retrieved May 9, 2020, from *https://resources. depaul.edu/abcd-institute/Pages/default.aspx*

Baker, A. (n.d. 2019, June 14). Why you should develop a coaching culture within your organization. *HR Professionals Magazine*. *https://hrprofessionalsmagazine.com/2019/06/14/why-you-should-develop-a-coaching-culture-within-your-organization/*

Bariso, J. (2017, April 24). Microsoft's CEO just gave some brilliant career advice. Here it is in 1 sentence. *Inc. https://www.inc.com/ justin-bariso/microsofts-ceo-just-gave-some-brilliant-career-advice-here-it-is-in-one-sentence.html*

Batista, E. (2015, February 18). How great coaches ask, listen, and empathize. *Harvard Business Review. https://hbr.org/2015/02/how-great-coaches-ask-listen-and-empathize*

Berglas, S. (2002, June). The very real dangers of executive coaching. *Harvard Business Review. https://hbr.org/2002/06/the-very-real-dangers-of-executive-coaching*

Boyatzis, R. (n.d.). What great coaching looks like [Audio podcast episode]. In *HBR IdeaCast*. https://hbr.org/podcast/2019/09/what-great-coaching-looks-like

Boyatzis, R. E., Smith, M., & Oosten, E. V. (2019, September/October). Coaching for change. *Harvard Business Review https://hbr. org/2019/09/coaching-for-change*

Boyatzis, R., Smith, Melvin, & Van Ossten, E. (2019). *Helping people change: Coaching with compassion for lifelong learning and growth*. Harvard Business Press.

Busse, D. (2017, February 14). The two types of business coaching. *Essential Impact*. *https://essentialimpact.com/blog/the-two-types-of-business-coaching/*

Cocivera, T. (2018, September 17). What does a coaching culture look like? *Forbes*. https://www.forbes.com/sites/forbescoachescouncil/2018/09/17/what-does-a-coaching-culture-look-like/

Covey, S. R. (1989). *The 7 habits of highly effective people: Powerful lessons in personal change*. Fireside.

Duckworth, A. (2016). *Grit: The power of passion and perseverance*. Scribner.

Dweck, C. (2006). *Mindset: The new psychology of success*. Ballantine Books.

Halvorson, H. G. (2011). *Succeed: How we can reach our goals*. Plume. *https://www.amazon.com/Succeed-How-Can-Reach-Goals/dp/0452297710*

Halvorson, H. G. (2012). *Nine things successful people do differently*. Harvard Business Review Press.

Harkavy, D. S. (2010). *Becoming a coaching leader: The proven system for building your own team of champions*. Thomas Nelson.

Ibarra, H., & Scoular, A. (2019, November/December). The leader as coach. *Harvard Business Review*. *https://hbr.org/2019/11/the-leader-as-coach*

Joo, B.-K. (Brian), Sushko, J. S., & McLean, G. N. (2012). Multiple faces of coaching: Manager-as-coach, executive coaching, and formal mentoring. *Organization Development Journal; Chesterland, 30*(1), 19–38.

Katz, L. (2020, February 12). The ultimate guide to open-ended questions vs. closed-ended questions. *ClearVoice*. *https://www.clearvoice.com/blog/open-ended-questions-vs-closed-questions/*

Kimsey-House, H. (2011). *Co-active coaching: Changing business, transforming lives* (3rd ed.). Nicholas Brealey Publishing.

Kotter, J. (2012). *Leading change*. Harvard Business Review Press.

Lencioni, P. (2012). *The advantage: Why organizational health trumps everything else in business*. Jossey-Bass.

Mann, R. (2019a). *Building strategic organizations: The first five tools for strategy and strategic planning*. ClarionStrategy.

Mann, R. (2019b). *Strategic leaders are made, not born: The first five tools for escaping the tactical tsunami*. ClarionStrategy.

Mann, R., & Tarrant, D. (2020). *Strategic finance for strategic leaders: The first five tools*. Clarion.

Mauri, T. (2019, February 4). Want to think like Satya Nadella? Follow 3 simple rules. *Inc.* https://www.inc.com/terence-mauri/how-satya-nadella-uses-learn-it-all-to-beat-know-it-all.html

McChesney, C., Covey, S., & Huling, J. (2016). *The 4 disciplines of execution: Achieving your wildly important goals* (Reprint ed.). Free Press.

McLean, P. (2012). *The completely revised handbook of coaching: A developmental approach* (2nd ed.). Jossey-Bass.

McLean, P. (2019). *Self as coach, self as leader*. Wiley.

Schmidt, E., Rosenberg, J., & Eagle, A. (2019). *Trillion dollar coach: The leadership playbook of Silicon Valley's Bill Campbell*. Harper Business.

Stanier, M. B. (2016). *The coaching habit: Say less, ask more & change the way you lead forever*. Box of Crayons Press.

Stoltzfus, T. (2008). *Coaching questions: A coach's guide to powerful asking skills* (1st edition). Coach22 Bookstore LLC.

United States Department of Agriculture (n.d.). *Differences between coaching, counseling, managing, mentoring, consulting and training*. https://www.dm.usda.gov/employ/vu/coaching-diff.htm

Warren, R. (2012). *The purpose driven life: What on earth am I here for?* Zondervan.

Webb, K. (2016, July 11). What it really means to be a coach. *Keith Webb. https://keithwebb.com/what-really-means-to-be-coach/*

Webb, K. (2019). *The coach model for Christian leaders: Powerful leadership skills for solving problems, reaching goals, and developing others*. Morgan James Faith.

Wickman, G. (2012). *Traction: Get a grip on your business* (Reprint ed. edition). BenBella Books.

ABOUT THE AUTHOR

Rick Mann, PhD, has served in a number of leadership roles across a wide variety of industries. He currently serves as Professor of Leadership and Strategy as well as Program Director for the MBA and DBA programs at Trevecca Nazarene University. In the past, he has served as the President and Provost of Crown College (MN), a program director in China, an executive coach, and a coaching trainer. His areas of interest and expertise begin with a passion for helping leaders and organizations to access and leverage the best thinking in strategy-making and leadership development today. This passion extends to his research and writing in the areas of strategy, strategic planning, coaching, and leadership development.

Over more than two decades, Rick has done extensive coaching and consulting with leaders, senior teams, and organizations whose budgets have ranged from $100K to $500 million. Rick has an MDiv from Ambrose University (Canada), an MBA from the University of Minnesota, and an MA and PhD from Ohio State University. He is also an Associate Certified Coach through the International Coach Federation (ICF).

CPSIA information can be obtained
at www.ICGtesting.com
Printed in the USA
BVHW031722161122
652141BV00007B/76